# GUGGENHEIM INTERNATIONAL EXHIBITION 1967

## SCULPTURE FROM TWENTY NATIONS

Distributed to the Trade by

D. VAN NOSTRAND COMPANY, INC.
Princeton, New Jersey

THE SOLOMON R. GUGGENHEIM MUSEUM

NEW YORK

OCTOBER 20, 1967—FEBRUARY 4, 1968


ART GALLERY OF ONTARIO

TORONTO

FEBRUARY—MARCH, 1968


THE NATIONAL GALLERY OF CANADA

OTTAWA

APRIL—MAY, 1968


MONTREAL MUSEUM OF FINE ARTS

MONTREAL

JUNE—AUGUST, 1968

The Guggenheim International Exhibitions had their origin in 1956. While all previous shows of this series presented surveys of painting, the subject of the current selection is sculpture.

The hopes for the Exhibitions have been from the outset that they would be significant in the field of art and also would be an important manifestation of international good will. The methods and rules for the Guggenheim Internationals have been modified over the years as we have sought constantly to find a formula that would achieve these objectives as nearly as possible.

In the current show, there are two major departures: one is the abandonment of a rigid system of national quotas; the other is the substitution of purchase awards for the originally established prize structure. The mode of selection has also changed over the years in our constant search for improvement.

This Fifth Guggenheim International Exhibition was staged by Thomas M. Messer, the Museum's Director, who in turn drew upon extensive advice and assistance. The exhibition project has been completed in cooperation with leading Canadian museums under whose auspices it will be presented, following the inauguration in New York, during the spring and summer months of 1968.

Harry F. Guggenheim, President      The Solomon R. Guggenheim Foundation

# LENDERS TO THE EXHIBITION

*Artists lending their own works are not listed below.*

Richard Brown Baker, New York
Richard Bellamy, New York
Paul and Timothy Caro, London
Mr. and Mrs. Wilfred P. Cohen, New York
Estate of Frederick Kiesler
Estate of David Smith
Mr. and Mrs. Arnold B. Glimcher, New York
Noah Goldowsky, New York
Miss Sarah Dora Greenberg, New York
Joseph H. Hirshhorn Collection
Aimé Maeght, Paris
Algur H. Meadows, Dallas
Mr. and Mrs. David L. Paul, New York
Kenneth Schnitzer, Houston
Mr. and Mrs. Rudolph B. Schulhof, Kings Point, New York

Stedelijk Museum, Amsterdam
Albright-Knox Art Gallery, Buffalo
The Museum of Fine Arts, Houston
Kyoto Municipal Museum of Art, Kyoto
Storm King Art Center, Mountainville, New York

Galleria dell'Ariete, Milan
Galerie Claude Bernard, Paris
Leo Castelli Gallery, New York
Galerie Chalette, New York
Cordier and Ekstrom, Inc., New York
Ferus Gallery, Los Angeles
Fischbach Gallery, New York
Robert Fraser Gallery, London
Gimpel Fils, Ltd., London
The Graham Gallery, New York
Galerie Alexandre Iolas, Paris
Sidney Janis Gallery, New York
Lefebre Gallery, New York
Galerie Maeght, Paris
Marlborough Galleria d'Arte, Rome
Marlborough-Gerson Gallery, New York
Galería Juana Mordó, Madrid
Galerie Müller, Stuttgart
Pace Gallery, New York
Park Place Gallery, New York
Betty Parsons Gallery, New York
Perls Galleries, New York
Stephen Radich Gallery, New York
Galerie Denise René, Paris
Rowan Gallery, London
Tokyo Gallery, Tokyo
Galerie van de Loo, Munich
Nicholas Wilder Gallery, Los Angeles
Galerie Renée Ziegler, Zürich

# ACKNOWLEDGEMENTS

*A sculpture survey is a complex undertaking based upon the creative and technical contributions rendered by many qualified individuals over a prolonged period of time. Determination of a policy framework by the President and Trustees of the Foundation preceded its implementation by the Director and the Staff of this Museum. A search for new talent and a reevaluation of established reputations—all within limits of availability of the desired works—were the two main processes of the preparatory stage. Eventually a logistic situation of considerable magnitude, beginning with the assembling of material from widely scattered parts of the world and ending with installation and presentation details, devolved upon the professional staffs.*

*The world-wide search for specific works has been assigned to Edward Fry, and it is on the basis of his findings furthered by artists, collectors, dealers, museum officials, and generally of individuals with special closeness to the subject that final decisions were reached. Mr. Fry therefore deserves much credit for exhaustive preparatory work while the undersigned accepts ultimate responsibility for commissions and omissions alike.*

*We are deeply indebted to all lenders whose names are separately listed. While it is impossible to acknowledge the very numerous contributions made toward this project during the past three years, the following individuals are listed because of the extensiveness of their help and assistance: Mr. Kazuo Akane, Kobe; Mr. Božo Bek, Zagreb; Mr. Richard Bellamy, New York; Dr. László Bényi, Budapest; Mr. Irving Blum, Los Angeles; Mr. Alan Bowness, London; Mr. Wieslaw Borowski, Warsaw; Mr. J. W. Borcoman, Ottawa; Mr. David Brooke, Toronto; Donna Carla Castelbarco, Milan; Professor Herschel Chipp, Berkeley; Mr. Ješa Denegri, Belgrade; Mr. Gillo Dorfles, Milan; Mr. Donald Droll, New York; Mr. Akio Fujieda, Kyoto; Mr. José Maria Moreno Galvan, Madrid; Dr. Werner Hofmann, Vienna; Mme. Vera Horvat-Pintarić, Zagreb; Mr. Pål Hougen, Oslo; Mr. Atsuo Imaizumi, Kyoto; Mr. Knud Jensen, Humlebaek; Mr. Zoran Kržišnik, Ljubljana; Mr. Tamon Miki, Tokyo; Baronessa Beatrice Monte della Corti, Milan; Mr. Edo Murtič, Zagreb; Mr. Yusuke Nakahara, Tokyo; Mr. Denraburo Nakamura, Tokyo; Contessa Carla Panicali, Rome; Mr. Alejandro Cirici-Pellicer, Barcelona; Mr. Miodrag Protić, Belgrade; Miss Jasia Reichardt, London; M. Pierre Restany, Paris; Mr. John Russell, London; Dr. Jiří Šětlik, Prague; Mr. Ryszard Stanislawski, Warsaw; Mr. Herman Swart, Amsterdam; Miss Beate Sydhoff, Stockholm; Mme. Gizela Szancerowa, Warsaw; Mr. Yoshiaki Tono, Yokohama; Mr. Maurice Tuchman, Los Angeles; Mr. Takashi Yamamoto, Tokyo.*

*The preparation of an exhibition and of an accompanying catalog of the scope and magnitude here described involves more than the usual exertion of curatorial and technical museum departments. Their work on all levels is therefore acknowledged here with much grateful awareness of its full extent. This Fifth Guggenheim International is co-sponsored by leading Canadian Museums and it is therefore my privilege to thank the Directors of The National Gallery of Canada in Ottawa, the Art Gallery of Ontario in Toronto, and the Montreal Museum of Fine Arts for their patient and valuable cooperation.*

*Thomas M. Messer, Director*                         *The Solomon R. Guggenheim Museum*

# PREFACE

The Guggenheim Internationals are attempts to gather the best recently produced works of art from available sources. As an objective, this would hardly seem open to discussion. As a procedural outline, however, such an aim is meaningless unless it is further defined within a set of prevailing circumstances. To begin with, *the best* is a vague concept. It has neither size, nor age, nor origin and lends itself to the most diverse and contradictory interpretations. To deal with it at all, the proposition must be narrowed from the outset to entities that may be meaningfully compared. Thus the Fifth Guggenheim International Exhibition with which we are here concerned is restricted to sculpture; it spans the years since 1960; and, it is meant to reflect creative attainments throughout the world. The exhibition framework thus rests on three determining elements —time, medium and scope.

The established *time-span* has implications beyond its seven years' duration. It comprises first, the works of artists who have helped to shape the sculptural identity of the 20th century decades ago and whose creative contributions have continued into the current decade. For exhibition purposes this old master label applies to sculptors born before 1910. A mid-generation, whose birthdays fall between 1910 and 1925 and which has in many instances made its most vital contributions in the years covered by this survey, follows chronologically. Lastly, and in some ways most importantly, there are the directions indicated by contemporary practitioners who, born after 1925, are today in their early forties at the most. Thus three creative generations each relatable within itself meet in the period under consideration. Engaged in simultaneous activity, each reflects very different pre-suppositions and expresses through its work ideals, aspirations and sensibilities that cannot be compared meaningfully within a single standard.

Even more problematical than the time variant is the application of the term "sculpture", *the artist's medium*. There was a time when everyone knew what sculpture meant. A solid and static three-dimensional object, it stood in space and thereby was clearly different in kind from the flat, square or rectangular surfaces that signified painting. In the 1960's many artists have exceeded such separations by creating modes that do not fit inherited categories. Painting, once a flat art, may now bulge forward, thereby shedding its attributes without necessarily embracing the sculptural alternative. The once solid masses of sculpture now are pierced and perforated. Solidity is further reduced through translucent surfaces which, together with materials borrowed from the modern industrial scene, have begun to replace the traditional wood, stone, and metal. Motion has added itself as a formal component in "kinetic art" and artificial light sources are enriching the vocabulary as "optical art". The sculptural object which until recently lived easily within prevailing definitions has slid down from its pedestal to confront us in material ambiguity, to confuse us with diminished solidity, often abandoning static calm for gentle or convulsive motion, and flickering at times before our eyes as color and light widen the artist's formal repertoire. Proclaiming its unconcern with "beauty" contemporary experimentation stresses its intent to use every possible means to manifest thought and to create material equivalents of a new and complex awareness. Since sculpture as it was known has been transcended by such developments, the question arises where the limits of sculpture are—a question that can only be answered arbitrarily and for the limited purposes of a specific occasion.

The exhibition's *international scope* also poses interesting dilemmas since geographical limitlessness upon close scrutiny shows itself as an inverted limit. While the search for sculpture of quality encompassed all accessible parts of the world, *the best* has been observed to concentrate itself in a relatively few centers in which the necessary technical, mechanical and spiritual pre-conditions for the exercise of sculpture prevail. An international style has become a firmly established notion in our time. This means the near-elimination of national characteristics and their displacement by a worldwide identity of creative aims. The result of such homogeneity of purpose is a self-engendered standard which rejects as irrelevant other theoretically imaginable measures of excellence. If, therefore, the sculpture gathered from a world-wide spectrum may lay claim to qualitative superiority, it is not so much because of its technical perfection, nor as a result of its expressive strength, but because of a demonstrated capacity to partake in an exchange of sculptured thought that through its implicit meanings engages the creative attention of those conversant with the language of forms.

Seen in this light, *the best* becomes a personal and, therefore, a fallible choice of about one hundred available works that conform to a pragmatic definition of the medium of sculpture—works searched out in accessible and plastically engaged parts of the world and created within two thirds of this century's seventh decade. National categories have not been stressed in this exhibition. Instead existing uniformities within each generation have been given more emphasis than they usually receive. Sculpture, for the purposes at hand, has been defined in an orthodox sense with emphasis upon its representative and material origins, and to the exclusion of "post-sculptural developments" which deserve a separate and full presentation and quite possibly another name. Style, to the degree to which it emerges, must be comprehended broadly as an inevitable mark of our age rather than as a similarity in mode or an identity of idiom.

Finally it should be stated that no exhibition is made in or for a vacuum and that this selection, like any other museum choice has been adjusted to a scale and a scope prescribed by the structure and the dimensions of the recipient institution—in this case the spiral ramps and the adjoining spaces of the Guggenheim Museum.

T.M.M.

# INTRODUCTION

by EDWARD F. FRY

Inevitably, a definition of sculpture *per se*, if only implicit and subject to revisions, must enter into an appraisal of its contemporary achievements. An approach suitable for dealing with sculpture previous to the beginning of the twentieth-century is inadequate for its more recent history, and this disparity increases as one draws nearer to the present. The interchangeability of solid and void, a long established tradition of twentieth-century sculpture, has devalued all previous criteria based on the idea of mass in favor of those relating to space; it is the means by which space, not mass, is treated that characterize modern sculpture. Similarly the sculptor's traditional materials of stone, bronze, and wood, as well as the techniques long associated with them, have ceased to occupy the unique role which was once theirs. An even more important change has occurred in the function of sculpture. Until the later nineteenth century the ends toward which sculpture was directed were either commemorative, with portraits and monuments; or symbolic, as in sculpture with mythological, religious, or historical content. These functions for sculpture, with the exception of portraiture, were already in decline by the last quarter of the nineteenth century, and during the first half of the twentieth have survived only in rare instances, there considerably modified and attenuated.

Long before the 1960's, however, twentieth-century sculptors were increasingly directing their works toward new symbolic ends, centering on aesthetics itself, such as propositions concerning three-dimensional perception; the creative process; principles of composition and the relations of color, volume, planes, and lines to each other; and speculations on the nature and role of a work of art. These ends now constitute the principal function of contemporary sculpture. The central issue, however, common to sculpture of today as well as of the past, remains a symbolic organization of space, by which sculpture becomes sculpture and not a disguised version of either painting or architecture.

Many of the younger generation of sculptors have begun their careers as painters, and the problem often emerges as to whether a given work is painting or sculpture. Usually such borderline situations are resolved through consideration of whether or not the work in question depends on the frontal development of a plane: if the total perception of such a work may be accomplished from a frontal vantage point, and this perception leads to the comprehension of the work as a two-dimensional pattern underlying and controlling any projections or extensions into space, the work is within the domain of painting.

The existence of doubt, however, indicates that a classification by two or three dimensions, though possible, is secondary if not irrelevant to the artist's principal intention. In such cases, this intention is usually either *stylistic*, concerned with the development of formal motifs and compositional methods, and the manipulation of line and color; or *iconographic*, in which the communication of certain images or symbols is the artist's overriding interest. In either instance the medium is of secondary importance and becomes a matter of the artist's conscious or unconscious choice.

Recently the division between sculpture and architecture has also become blurred through the development of "environmental" sculpture; and here the distinction, although of considerable importance, is somewhat more difficult to make. Almost all good architecture has sculptural qualities; thus, a work of contemporary sculpture sometimes resembles an architectural model. But architecture also necessarily possesses two qualities foreign to sculpture: large scale relative to the human body, and social utility or function. Even the most ambitiously environmental sculpture cannot claim both of these qualities and in fact is usually closely tied to a human scale.

Many contemporary artists have reacted against the conception of sculpture as a rare or precious object, mounted on a pedestal to symbolize an ideal separation from the world. Among the sculptors who reject this traditional position it has become a commonplace to create works which sit on the floor or ground without a pedestal, or which are attached directly to a wall or suspended from a ceiling. As noted above, one of the few limits which seem to operate, consciously or not, in such environmental sculpture is a cannily applied human module: the work is never at an exactly human scale and very rarely smaller. Nor is it often very much larger in scale than is necessary to avoid a confusion, in the perception of the spectator, with an image of the human body. These limitations of scale are curiously yet logically almost identical to those in Hellenic and Renaissance classical sculpture.

When, however, the contemporary sculptor makes large works, with or without the conscious desire to create an environment, he enters a problematic realm of another order, in which the definition of the medium and its limits again becomes relevant: if a sculpture reaches a size large enough to fill a room or gallery, it is no longer simply sculpture, even if conceived in relation to the scale of the human body. At such a point sculpture crosses a boundary, beyond which lies either stage design or interior architecture. The breaching of this limit in recent years has often been highly productive over the short run: the extension of an artistic medium into unfamiliar territory always produces the tension of novelty during the period of its assimilation. After this stage, however, the artist must find yet further and possibly even more extreme means of challenging the nature of his medium, if he would continue to evoke the psychological climate of shock, tension, and novelty.

The hidden motivation within this recent exploitation of scale and limit in sculpture is the artist's unwillingness to continue working within the context of existing formalist styles, most of the potentialities of which have already been realized and which are fast becoming clichés of design. Barring the almost insuperable problem of creating a new and compelling iconography, the most tempting path for many sculptors is formalist invention coupled with large scale. Even these innovations are in many instances new versions of old geometries or design problems, and will eventually revert to their original status as cliché, once the disguise of dramatic size has been penetrated and discounted.

The conception of sculpture and of its limits, as indicated above, is intended as a point of departure for situating the intentions of contemporary artists within a broad framework. The consequences of such a norm for sculpture might appear to be self-defeating, if an increasing number of sculptors were to make it irrelevant and thereby proclaim the end of sculpture in any strict sense—an event that would signal changes of extreme importance in culture and society were it to occur. There are in fact indications that the cultural function of sculpture may at some future date be absorbed in large part by aspects of architecture, design and technology.

At present, however, sculpture remains a highly fertile and inventive medium; and the range of possibilities and limits suggested for it here is not only relevant to its contemporary achievements but also useful in clarifying the innovations of post-sculptural art, as well as those of artists using light and movement. Thus, most light and kinetic art, even if nominally presented in a three-dimensional format, resolves itself into a two-dimensional pattern or sequence of patterns. A few kinetic artists, notably Alexander Calder, Jean Tinguely, George Rickey, and Pol Bury, use movement to articulate space or to create metaphor; they are sculptors and should be considered as such. A somewhat greater number of artists use movement in order to explore and map its potentialities and are neither painters nor sculptors, but true kineticists.

If one examines the general situation of sculpture today (and of painting as well) the most striking facts to emerge are, first, that the best and most advanced work is being done in a relatively small number of places. Sculpture, even more than poetry, is a cultural luxury; and because of the relatively great expense involved in its production, it flourishes today almost always in large cities supported by rich and highly developed technological societies—New York, London, Tokyo, Los Angeles, Düsseldorf, Milan, Paris. It is further remarkable that with few exceptions the English-speaking peoples exert a sculptural hegemony over the rest of the world.

In the case of Great Britain, Henry Moore and Barbara Hepworth maintain their positions as salient figures in a national sculptural renaissance which they inaugurated. The work of both continues to be based on an uneasy and fluctuating amalgam of late cubist anthropomorphism with a romantic philosophy or organicism and vitalism. Although the precise tenets of this philosophy are elusive, they revolve about the idea, felt more than thought, that sculpture should reflect the forms and processes of natural life and that consequently the sculptor will be able to capture the essence of organic life within the inert material of his works. The immediately succeeding generation of English sculptors remain prominent through the works of William Turnbull, Eduardo Paolozzi, and Anthony Caro. During the 1960's all have rejected the humanist-vitalist tenets of Moore, with varying degrees of urgency and persuasiveness; this rejection was not accomplished immediately, but tentatively and in a more or less empirical fashion. It was Caro, significantly a former assistant to Moore, who at the beginning of the 1960's led the way in turning from traditional materials and methods and in exploring new modes of both the composition and presentation of sculpture. The younger British sculptors, of whom Phillip King and William Tucker are representative talents, have gone even further than their predecessors in a categorical rejection of the past; and their preoccupation with environmental and conceptual problems links them closely to their American contemporaries.

By contrast, sculptors in Western Europe, and particularly in France, seem for the moment at least to be concerned more with restating and developing the cubist, constructivist, or surrealist-expressionist innovations of their early twentieth-century predecessors, rather than with attempting fundamentally new approaches to sculpture. In such a situation, the predecessors themselves often continue to dominate the artistic life of their country, as is true, for example, of Marino Marini and Lucio Fontana in Italy. Within this somewhat circumscribed but nevertheless vital European tradition, the highly individualistic talents of Étienne-Martin, Jean Ipousteguy and Piotr Kowalski in France, Eduardo Chillida in Spain, and Pol Bury in Belgium emerge as outstanding examples of the possibilities for renewal and extension of a previously established artistic framework.

The most rapidly developing center of contemporary art is Japan; it is also the least known, notwithstanding attempts in recent years to familiarize Western audiences with its representative talents. Japan today has with few exceptions only one generation of artists of interest, almost all of whom are under forty. Within this group has appeared a significant number of sculptors who are independent both of traditional Japanese art and of eclectic subservience to current occidental styles. Of these, Morio Shinoda, Katsuhiro Yamaguchi, Noriyasu Fukushima, Ken Sakaki, and Kazuo Yuhara are among the outstanding figures, combining technical brilliance and imaginative utilization of new materials with formal invention of a high order. The best work of these sculptors possesses by a kind of secret birthright the post-classical, non-anthropomorphic qualities achieved with such self-conscious and deliberate effort on the part of young British and American sculptors.

Much of the most radically innovative sculpture in the world today is being produced in the United States, primarily in New York but also in Los Angeles, with an increasingly important exchange developing between these two centers. The sheer quantity and diversity of work being produced throughout the country preclude any overall characterization of American sculpture as a whole. Undoubtedly there is a more intense experimentation with new materials, forms, and stylistic ideas in the United States than may be found elsewhere, as is true also of the speed and intensity with which advanced artistic problems are posed and resolved. However, to compare either sculpture or painting in America with that in Europe or Great Britain, or even within the United States to differentiate between artists in California, on the eastern seaboard, or in other areas, is impossible except at the most general level of national or regional characterizations.

It is only in regard to the works of specific artists, seen within an ideological and historical context, that any pertinent comparisons or critical judgments may be made. But in America, as elsewhere in the world, the sequence and conflict of generations are of decisive importance to the understanding of the contemporary situation in sculpture. The works of today's international old masters, be they the late David Smith, Calder, Gabo, Nevelson, Marini, Moore, Lipchitz, or Picasso, reflect a latter-day continuation of earlier twentieth-century stylistic revolutions, particularly cubism and its expressionist or constructivist postludes. An immediately succeeding generation, comprising artists born generally although not exclusively between 1910 and 1930, underwent a strong reaction against its predecessors: representative sculptors of this include Ipousteguy, Etienne-Martin, Tinguely, Caro, and the Americans Peter Agostini, Richard Stankiewicz, John Chamberlain, Mark Di Suvero, and George Segal. Characteristic of this generation is a selective rejection of its elders' stylistic preoccupations and a romantic obsession with private mythology, of which the principal ingredient is the myth of the artist's own creative process. Thus gesture, experimentation with new materials, technique, and the imprint of elapsed time, whether isolated or combined with a public or private iconography, become in many instances the essential content of the sculptor's work.

The present international generation of young sculptors in their twenties and thirities has continued the revolt of this middle generation by intensifying it to an extreme degree and thereby achieving both the freedom and the limitations of the *tabula rasa*—the clean slate upon which a totally new and independent art may be invented. It is on this common ground that sculptors so seemingly diverse as Tucker, Fukushima, Yuhara, and in the United States Donald Judd, John McCracken, Robert Morris, and Larry Bell meet and pursue parallel goals. Of these the most fundamental would seem to be the escape from history, a romantic attitude which in itself is a recurring characteristic of occidental culture since the beginning of the nineteenth century and hence destined in this current form also to become eventually an identifiable historical phenomenon.

To escape from history is also to escape from art history, which at least for today and the near future implies not only the escape from classical ideas of iconography, composition, and the relation of form to content, but also an escape from the recent past of modern art. Any taint or suggestion of earlier twentieth-century styles must therefore be avoided, and all indications of process eliminated. Hence the extreme preoccupation with either unitary and indivisible, or linear and repetitive, modes of composition: Tucker's parallel cylinders, Judd's repeated elements, McCracken's irreducible slab. In each case the relational, synthesizing compositional methods, basic to Western art from the Renaissance through cubism, have been bypassed. Hence also the almost universal preference of young sculptors for new, often synthetic materials, which possess none of the art-historical connotations of cast bronze or carved wood and stone. These materials, new to sculpture and often adapted from their roles in advanced contemporary technology, are almost always handled by the artist in such a way that in the final work no trace of the creative process is visible.

Fundamental to the ultimate artistic achievements of this contemporary version of the *tabula rasa* are two essential qualities. The first is the artist's capacity to originate clear and unifying concepts, arrived at not through a series of works or the gradual reduction of an idea to its essence, but directly and at the beginning: the conception of the work, be it Anthony Smith's black box or Fukushima's arch, must be completely realized before the work is made. Consequently the sculpture itself may often be partially or wholly executed by assistants, and frequently in a factory. The crucial factor thus resides ever more firmly in the quality of the original conception.

Brilliance of conception alone, however, is insufficient to prevent this mode of sculpture from disappearing into the limbo of the well-designed, well-proportioned object. The conception itself must be accompanied, and at least in part guided, by a distinct sensibility. This sensibility, which is the hidden but essential content of much of the new sculpture in England and America, guides the many choices concerning scale, material, and color posed by the realization of a work. At best, as in the art of Bell, Judd, McCracken, Morris, Tucker, and a very few others, the intensity and purity of the original concept may attain to the logic and power of a sign, exemplifying a sensibility or a state of mind yet eluding all attempts to reduce it either to pure symbol or sheer object. This state of mind is secular, post-metaphysical, and skeptical, and gives assent at most to a belief in a purely man-made, highly sensuous reality.

✳

The era may already be drawing to an irrevocable close in which art is focussed upon the creation of unique, tangible *objects*, to be exhibited and merchandised like other objects. There is already some evidence that a new conception of art is gathering force that will finally emerge to replace the art based in the sensuous and physical qualities of an object. This new art would be only incidentally tangible and serve as witness to the presence of intangible *systems*. At first it would incorporate various manifestations of energy, including light and movement; but eventually the path followed may be that of cybernetics. At present, however, there are only relatively primitive beginnings in this direction. Attempts to create flexible systems range from the static modular reliefs of Vjenceslav Richter to the relatively sophisticated efforts of a small but increasing number of cybernetic artists whose work already transcends even the broadest limits of any traditional conception of sculpture, such as is at issue here. The ultimate goal will be to fulfill the Faustian dream of creating life and intelligence itself; at which point the history of sculpture—be it that of prehistoric fertility images, of antique and Renaissance idealism, the organicism of Arp and Moore, or the kinetic art of Rickey and Tinguely—will have been consumated, and the myth of Pygmalion will have become fact.

The exhibition and the accompanying catalogue are divided into four parts as follows:

I.  artists who have died during the 1960's and whose work reaches significantly into the current decade

II.  artists born before 1910

III.  artists born between 1910 and 1925

IV.  artists born since 1925

# I

ARP

KIESLER

GIACOMETTI

DILLER

DAVID SMITH

KEMENY

**JEAN ARP**

Born 1887, Strassburg, Germany.
Died 1966, Basel, Switzerland.

Education: 1905-07, Kunstgewerbeschule, Weimar; 1908, Académie Julian, Paris. 1916-19, co-founder of Zurich Dada movement. 1925, participated in first Surrealist Group Exhibition, Galerie Pièrre, Paris. 1949-50, travelled in the United States. 1929, first one-man exhibition, Kunsthaus, Zurich. Awards: 1954, 1st International Sculpture Prize, XXVII Venice Biennale; 1963, Grand Prix National des Arts, Paris; 1964, Grand Prize, Landes Nordrhein-Westfalen, and Carnegie Award, Pittsburgh International Exhibition; 1965, Goethe Prize, University of Hamburg.

FRUIT OF A STONE. 1959-60.
Marble, H. 23½ x W. 43 x D. 19″.
Lent by Galerie Chalette, New York.
In the late 1950's, Arp made a small marble version of this work, based on another very small stone of the 1930's. The present work, executed in marble with the aid of assistants from an original full-scale plaster, represents the final development of these earlier versions and is unique in its present form.

**ARP**
FALLEN LEAF (FEUILLE SE REPOSANT). 1959-65.
Marble, H. 41½″, with marble base.
Lent by Sidney Janis Gallery, New York.
This unique marble derives from a similar small bronze of 1959; the
original plaster of this early bronze was used as the model from
which the later version was made, through the process of stereo-
metric enlargement known as "pointing." Arp himself subsequently
perfected the surfaces and configuration of the final marble.

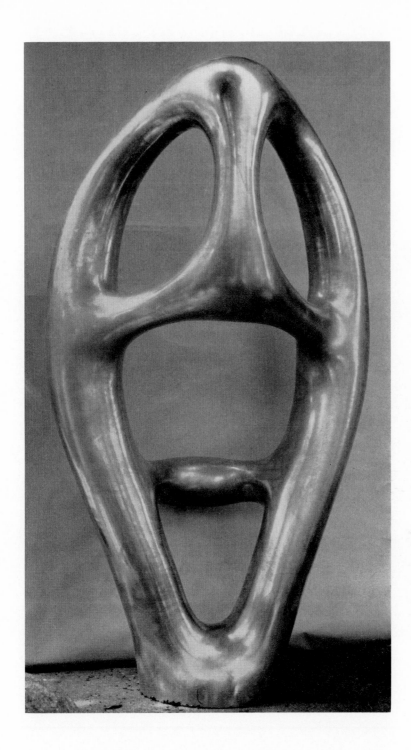

PTOLEMY III (PTOLEMÉE III). 1961.
Bronze, H. 79½".
Lent by Galerie Denise René, Paris.
For such large works in bronze, Arp made editions of three, using a
full-scale plaster model as a basis for casting by the lost wax process.

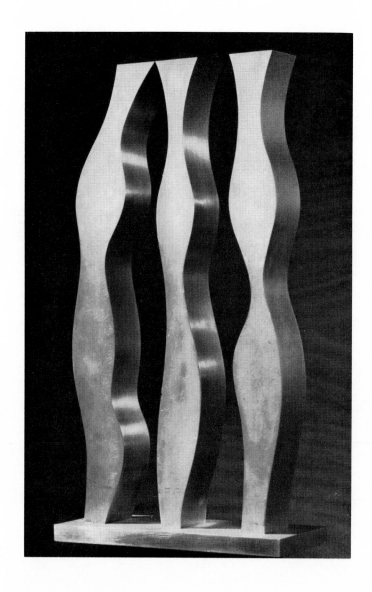

**ARP**      THREE GRACES (TROIS GRÂCES). 1961.
Wood and duraluminum, H. 20½".
Lent by Galerie Denise René, Paris.
When using duraluminum, Arp habitually made editions of 5 for
each work. Here as in other similar late works, the artist made sten-
cils which were used as the basis for a die to cut out the patterns in
metal, following which the elements were welded together.

THE MUSTACHE OF MACHINES
(LA MOUSTACHE DES MACHINES). 1965.
Bronze, H. 21¾″.
Lent by Galerie Denise René, Paris.
As in his works in duraluminum, Arp here used a stencil for cutting
the pattern in bronze, prior to the assembling and welding of the
final work.

**FREDERICK KIESLER**

Born 1896, Vienna.
Died 1965, New York.

Education: Akademie der Bildenden Künste, Vienna (M.A.);
Technische Hochschule, Vienna. 1923, designed first "endless house",
first stage design, and joined *De Stijl* group. 1926, New York.
Worked as architect, scenic designer, furniture designer. 1934-37,
Director of Scenic Design, Julliard School of Music. 1936, became
United States citizen. 1936-42, Director of the Laboratory for Design
Correlation of the School of Architecture, Columbia University.
1947, Paris. 1957, designed World House Galleries, New York. 1965,
dedication of "Shrine of the Book" (designed by Kiesler), Hebrew
University, Jerusalem.

DAVID. 1964-65. (right)                                    Detail (above)
Bronze, nickle bronze, stainless steel, H. 89 x W. 94 x D. 72".
Estate of the artist.

Cast posthumously by the raw sand process, in an edition of one only,
from the artist's orginal full scale maquette of plaster and cement.
*David* is part of Kiesler's last major work, a sculptural environment
48 feet in length entitled *Us, You, Me,* which depicts allegorically
the dilemma between action and meaning in the contemporary world.

## ALBERTO GIACOMETTI

Born 1901, Stampa, Switzerland.
Died, 1966, Chur (Coire), Switzerland.

Education: 1919-20, École des Arts et Métiers, Geneva; 1922-25, Académie de la Grande Chaumière, Paris. 1920, first trip to Italy. 1922, with Bourdelle in Paris. 1932, first one-man exhibition, Galerie Pierre Colle, Paris. Awards: 1960, Carnegie Award, Pittsburgh International Exhibition; 1962, Grand Prize for Sculpture, XXXI Venice Biennale; 1964, Guggenheim International Award for painting.

MAN WHO WALKS I (HOMME QUI MARCHE I). 1960. (3 views)
Bronze, H. 71¾".
Collection Albright-Knox Art Gallery, Buffalo, Gift of Seymour H. Knox.
Giacometti modelled almost all his late works in plaster or clay, from which editions of six bronzes were cast by the lost wax process.

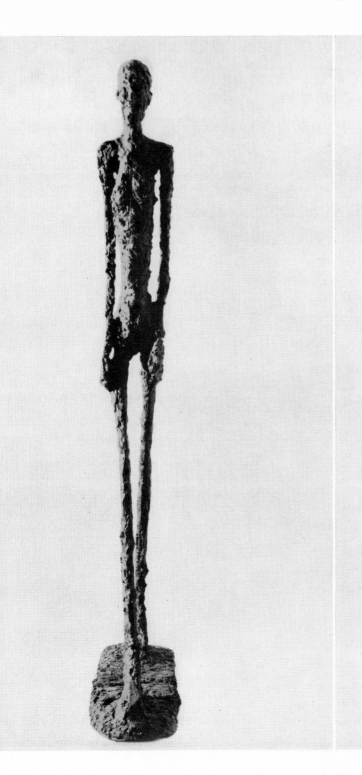 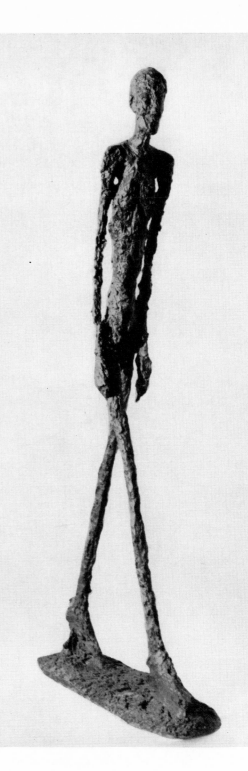

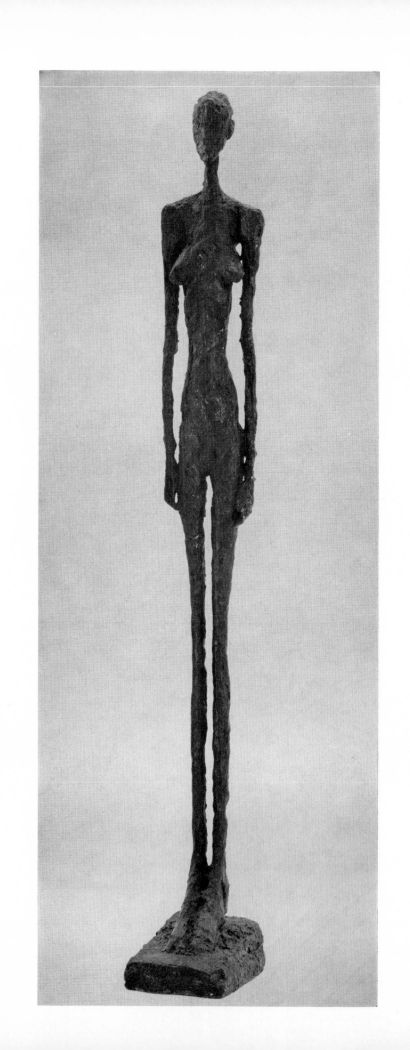

**GIACOMETTI**

STANDING WOMAN III (FEMME DEBOUT III). 1960.  (left)
Bronze, H. 92½″.
Lent by Marlborough-Gerson Gallery, New York.

BUST OF YANAIHARA (BUSTE DE YANAIHARA). 1961.  (above)
Bronze, H. 17″.
Collection Mr. and Mrs. Wilfred P. Cohen, New York.

**GIACOMETTI**     ANNETTE VIII. 1962.          ANNETTE IX. 1964.
Bronze, H. 23⅛″.              Bronze, H. 17½″.
Private collection.           Private collection.

CHIAVENNAN HEAD (TÊTE CHIAVENNA). 1965.
Bronze, H 16¼″.
Private collection.
Chiavenna is a town in Italy near the Swiss border.

**BURGOYNE DILLER**

Born 1906, New York.
Died 1965, New York.

Education: Michigan State University; Art Students League, New York. 1946, first one-man exhibition, Pinacotheca Gallery, New York. 1940-41, Head of Mural Division of the Federal Art Project, New York City; 1941-42, Director of New York City War Service Art Section, W.P.A.

PROJECT FOR GRANITE, NO. 1. 1963.
Formica, H. 84″.
Collection Noah Goldowsky and Richard Bellamy, New York.
All of Diller's sculptures were executed in formica by an industrial fabricating shop according to exact drawings and plans furnished by the artist.

**DILLER**

PROJECT FOR GRANITE, NO. 6. 1963.
Formica, H. 68¼″.
Collection Noah Goldowsky and Richard Bellamy, New York.

PROJECT FOR GRANITE, NO. 10. 1964.
Formica, H. 84″.
Collection Noah Goldowsky and Richard Bellamy, New York.

**DAVID SMITH**

Born 1906, Decatur, Indiana.
Died 1965, Albany, New York.

Education: 1924, Ohio University; 1926-30, Art Students League,
New York (studied with John Sloan and Jan Matulka). 1935, trav-
elled in U.S.S.R. and Europe. 1962, worked in Voltri and Spoleto,
Italy. 1938, first one-man exhibition, East River Gallery, New York.
Awards: 1950-51, Guggenheim Foundation Fellowship; 1964, Bran-
deis University Creative Arts Award.

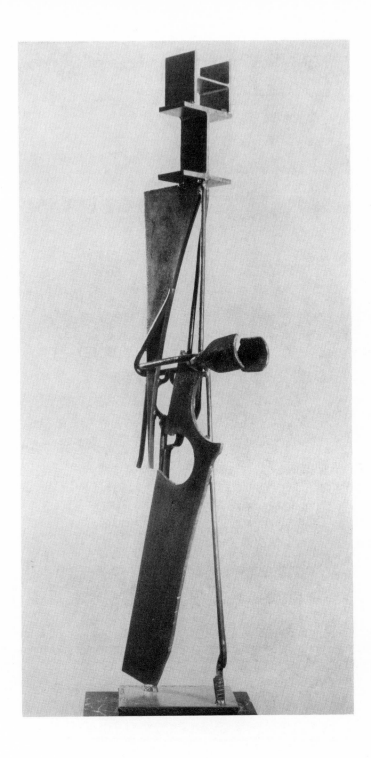

VOLTRI VIII. 1962. (left)
Steel, H. 79¼ x W. 40¾ x D. 32½".
Estate of the artist, courtesy Marlborough-Gerson Gallery, New York.
Like the other twenty-five sculptures made for the Spoleto Festival
during Smith's one month visit to Italy in 1962, this work was made
in an abandoned factory from fragments of steel which were cut and
bent, and then welded together. As is true of almost the entire Smith
oeuvre, this work exists in a unique version.

VOLTRON XV. 1963. (above)
Steel, H. 75 x W. 16 x D. 16".
Estate of the artist, courtesy Marlborough-Gerson Gallery, New York.
Welded together from steel scrap and foundry tools, incorporated as
*objets trouvés*.

**DAVID SMITH**

VB XXIII. 1963.  (above)
Steel, H. 69½ x W. 24 x D. 25½″.
Collection Miss Sarah Dora Greenberg, New York.
A welded assemblage of scrap steel.

CUBI XXVII. 1965.  (right)
Stainless steel, H. 111⅜ x W. 87¾ x D. 34″.
Estate of the artist, courtesy Marlborough-Gerson Gallery, New York.
In the late Cubi series Smith continued his use of welded assemblage, but resorted to more careful planning of composition through preliminary drawings, collages, and trial assembling. The stainless steel surfaces, once welded together, were then roughly buffed to give them a variegated irridescent sheen.

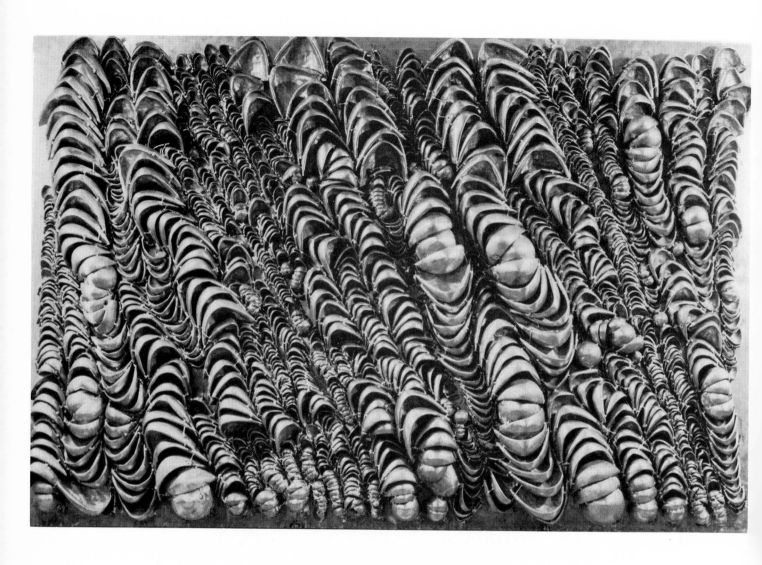

## ZOLTAN KEMENY

Born 1907, Banica, Transylvania.
Died 1965, Zurich, Switzerland.

Education: 1924-27, École des Arts Décoratifs, Budapest (studied architecture) ; 1927-30, École des Beaux-Arts, Budapest (studied painting). 1930-40, Paris ; 1940-42, Marseille ; 1942, Zurich. 1950, became Swiss citizen.

VISUALIZATION OF THE INVISIBLE
(VISUALISATION DE L'INVISIBLE). 1960.
Brass, H. 72½ x W. 106″.
Joseph H. Hirshhorn Collection.
Kemeny's working method here, as almost always during the 1960's, was to solder together strips and pieces of brass which he had previously bent to the desired shape.

IMAGE WITH FOUR SIDES
(IMAGE À QUATRE FACES). 1962.
Iron, copper, wood H. 27¾".
Lent by Galerie Maeght, Paris.

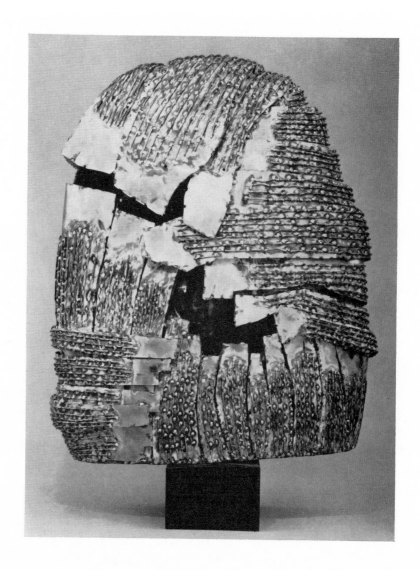

**KEMENY**     THE BELL (LA CLOCHE). 1964.
Brass, H. 30½″.
Lent by Galerie Maeght, Paris.
Soldered brass assemblage.

ZEPHYR (ZÉPHYR). 1964.
Brass, colored polyester (relief), H. 53 x W. 42½".
Lent by Galerie Maeght, Paris.
Brass and plastic elements, soldered together and attached to a sup-
porting panel.

# II

PICASSO

LIPCHITZ

CALDER

MOORE

COLLA

FONTANA

NEVELSON

MARINI

HEPWORTH

NOGUCHI

RICKEY

WOTRUBA

BILL

MANZU

## PABLO PICASSO

Born 1881, Malaga, Spain.
Residence Mougins, France.

1895, moved to Barcelona. Education: 1897, École des Beaux-Arts, Barcelona; Académie Royale des Beaux-Arts, Madrid. 1900-01, trips to Madrid and Paris. 1904, settled in Paris. 1901, first one man exhibition Galerie Ambrose Vollard, Paris. Awards: 1962, Lenin Peace Prize; Honorary Citizen of Antibes.

STANDING WOMAN (FEMME DEBOUT). 1961.
Sheet iron, polychromed, H. 70 x W. 67".
Collection The Museum of Fine Arts, Houston; Gift from the Esther Florence Whinery Goodrich Foundation.
Picasso's recent series of sculpture in sheet iron, of which this work is a part, were made by metal workers and craftsmen who followed small-scale cut-out sketches which the artist prepared with scissors and paper. This particular work, which exists in two versions, was also the source for a similar monumental sculpture in concrete realized in 1961-62.

**JACQUES LIPCHITZ**

Born 1891, Druskieniki, Lithuania.
Residence Hastings-on-Hudson, New York.

Education: 1909-11, Académie des Beaux-Arts, Paris (studied with
Jean Antoine Ingalbert and Dr. Richet); Académie Julian, Paris
(studied with Raoul Verlet); Académie Colarossi, Paris. 1924, be-
came French citizen. 1941, came to United States. Travelled in
Europe, Middle East, United States. 1920, first one-man exhibition,
Galerie de l'Effort Moderne (Léonce Rosenberg), Paris. Awards:
1909, First Prize for Sculpture, Académie Julian, Paris; 1937, Gold
Medal, Paris World's Fair; 1946, French Legion of Honor; 1952,
George D. Widener Memorial Gold Medal, Pennsylvania Academy of
Fine Arts; 1958, Honorable D.F.A., Brandeis University; 1966, Gold
Medal, American Academy of Arts and Letters, New York.

GOVERNMENT OF THE PEOPLE. 1967.
Bronze, H. 51″.
Lent by Marlborough-Gerson Gallery, New York.
Lipchitz's preferred working method, used here and for the past
40 years, is to model in plaster from which a bronze cast is made by
the lost wax method; Lipchitz retouches the wax model for each
cast. The usual edition of his works comprises seven casts; but this
work, being the artist's one-sixth scale model for a major monument
for the city of Philadelphia, will exist in two casts only, of which this
is the first.

## ALEXANDER CALDER

Born 1898, Philadelphia.
Residence Roxbury, Connecticut, and Saché
(Indre-et-Loire), France.

Education: 1915-19, Stevens Institute of Technology; 1923-26, Art Students League, New York (studied with George Luks, Guy du Bois, Boardman Robinson and John Sloan). Travelled in Europe, United States, Latin America, India. 1928, Paris. 1928, first one-man exhibition, Weyhe Gallery, New York. Awards: 1952, First Prize, XXVI Venice Biennale; 1953, II São Paulo Bienal; 1956, Medal, Stevens Institute of Technology; 1958, Carnegie Award, Pittsburgh International Exhibition; 1960, Gold Medal, Architectural League of New York; 1962, Brandeis University, Creative Arts Award.

SPIRAL (MOTORIZED STANDING MOBILE). 1966. (left)
Steel with motorized elements, H. 118″.
Lent by Perls Galleries, New York.
Constructed industrially from plans and drawings of the artist and under his supervision. The spiral both girates and oscillates, at various speeds and in reverse as well as forward. Its motions are powered by two separate motors that are controlled and synchronized by a flexibly programmed electronic regulator.

TOM'S CUBICLE. 1967. (above)
Steel, H. 120 x W. 146 x D. 79″.
Lent by Perls Galleries, New York.

**HENRY MOORE**

Born 1898, Castleford, Yorkshire.
Residence Much Hadham, Hertsfordshire.

Education: 1919, Leeds School of Art; 1921-26, Royal College of Art, London. 1923, visited Paris; 1925-26, spent six months visiting Paris and Italy. 1936, travelled in Spain; 1946, first visit to United States; 1951-58, trips to Greece, Brazil, Mexico, Italy, The Netherlands, Germany, Yugoslavia and Poland; 1958-65, trips to United States. 1928, first one-man exhibition, Warren Gallery, London. Awards: Honorary Doctorates, 1958, Harvard University; 1959, Cambridge University; 1961, Oxford University; 1966, Yale University; 1948, International Sculpture Prize, XXIV Venice Biennale: 1957, Stephan Lochner Medal, Cologne; 1958, Carnegie Award, Pittsburgh International Exhibition.

RECLINING FIGURE NO. 5. 1963-64.
Bronze, H. 96 x W. 150 x D. 72″.
Lent by the artist.
This work began as a small maquette which was then enlarged in two steps, with the aid of assistants, to a full scale plaster model, from which the bronze was cast by the lost-wax method. (Illustration shows the full scale plaster model.)

**ETTORE COLLA**

Born 1899, Parma, Italy.
Residence Rome.

Education: 1913-20, Accademia di Belle Arti, Parma. 1923, lived in
Paris and Brussels; 1924, Munich; 1926, Italy; 1928, visited Switzerland; 1934, London; 1935, Berlin. 1949, founded "Gruppo Origine".
1957, first one-man exhibition, Gallery "La Tartaruga", Rome.
Awards: 1937, Prize, International Exhibition "Arte e Tecnica",
Paris; 1939 won competition for Chair of Sculpture at Liceo Artis-
tico, Rome.

SOLAR WORKSHOP (OFFICINA SOLARE). 1964.
Iron, H. 84″.
Lent by the artist.
Welded assemblage of scrap iron and found objects.

**LUCIO FONTANA**

Born 1899, Rosario, Argentina.
Residence Milan.

1905, moved to Italy; 1921, returned to Argentina. Education: 1927-29, Brera Academy, Milan. 1936, Paris; 1939, returned to Argentina for war years; 1947, back to Milan; 1961, visited New York. 1930, first one-man exhibition, Galleria del Milione, Milan. From 1934, a member of Abstraction-Création Group. Awards: 1966, Grand Prize, XXXIII Venice Biennale.

SPATIAL IDEA (CONCETTO SPAZIALE). 1961.
Bronze, 4 spheres, c. 40″ diameter each; 1 sphere, c. 35″ diameter.
Joseph H. Hirshhorn Collection.
Cast by the lost wax method from the artist's original plaster models in an edition of two complete sets, of which this is the first.

**LOUISE NEVELSON**

Born 1900, Kiev, Russia.
Residence New York.

1905, immigrated to Rockland, Maine. Education: 1920, studied painting and drawing with Theresa Bernstein and William Meyerowitz; 1931, studied with Hans Hofmann, Munich. 1932, assistant to Diego Rivera on a mural for the New Workers' School, New York City. 1948, travelled in Europe (England, France, Italy); 1950, Mexico. 1953-55, studied under Peter Grippe and Leo Katz at *Atelier 17*, New York. 1941, first one-man exhibition, Nierendorf Gallery, New York. Awards: 1963, Fellowship at Tamarind Workshop, Los Angeles; 1966, Honorary Doctor of Fine Arts, Western College for Women, Oxford, Ohio.

ATMOSPHERE AND ENVIRONMENT VI. 1967.
Magnesium, black epoxy enamel, H. 102 x W. 96 x D. 48″.
Lent by Pace Gallery, New York.
Made by an industrial fabricator after a small-scale maquette and instructions furnished by the artist.

**MARINO MARINI**

Born 1901, Pistoia, Italy.
Residence Milan.

Education: Accademia di Belle Arti, Florence. 1943, visited Switzerland; 1950, New York for one month, visited England. 1932, first one-man exhibition Galleria Milano, Milan. Since 1940, teacher, Accademia Brera, Milan. Awards: 1935, Grand Prize, II Quadrennale, Romana; 1937, Sculpture Prize, World's Fair, Paris; 1952, Grand Prize for Sculpture, XXVI Venice Biennale; 1954, Feltrinelli Prize, Accademia dei Lincei, Rome.

COMPOSITION OF ELEMENTS
(COMPOSIZIONE DI ELEMENTI). 1964-65.
Bronze, H. 39¼ x W. 110¾ x D. 53½".
Collection Mr. and Mrs. Rudolph B. Schulhof, Kings Point, New York.
Marini usually makes three casts of his large bronzes, using the lost wax method based on an original model in plaster; this work, however, exists at present in but a single example.

**DAME BARBARA HEPWORTH**

Born 1903, Wakefield, Yorkshire.
Residence St. Ives, Cornwall, since 1939.

Education: Leeds School of Art; 1921, Royal College of Art, London. 1924-26, Italy; 1932, 1935, Paris; 1959, New York. 1928, first one-man exhibition, Beaux Arts Gallery, London. Awards: 1959, Grand Prize, V São Paulo Bienal; 1963, "The Foreign Ministers Award", 7th Tokyo Biennale; 1965, was created D.B.E. (Dame Commander of the Order of the British Empire).

THREE STANDING FORMS. 1965.
Stone, H. 69″.
Lent by Gimpel Fils, Ltd., London.
Carved directly in stone by the artist.

**ISAMU NOGUCHI**

Born 1904, Los Angeles, California.
Residence Long Island City, New York.

1906-20, Japan. Education: Columbia University (pre-medical);
apprenticed briefly to Gutzon Borglum; Leonardo da Vinci Art
School, New York; East Side Art School, New York. 1927-29, apprenticed to Constantin Brancusi, Paris. Travelled Mexico, U.S.S.R.,
the Orient, Europe, Israel, United States. 1929, first one-man exhibition, Eugene Schoen Gallery, New York. Awards: 1927, Guggenheim
Foundation Fellowship; 1950, Bollingen Foundation Fellowship;
Mr. and Mrs. Frank G. Logan Medal, The Art Institute of Chicago.

RESONANCE. 1966-67.
Marble, H. 24 x W. 66 x D. 22″ (with base).
Lent by Cordier and Ekstrom, Inc., New York.
Carved directly in stone by the artist.

**FRITZ WOTRUBA**

Born 1907, Vienna.
Residence Vienna.

Education: 1921-24, Vienna School of Fine Arts; 1926, School of
Anton Hanak; 1927, studied with Professor Steinhof. 1930, Germany, Holland (met Josef Hofmann); 1934, Zurich; 1937, Paris
(met Maillol); 1938-45, Switzerland; 1945, returned to Vienna
(taught at Akademie der Bildenden Künste); 1947, Rome and Paris;
1951, Munich, Brussels, Switzerland. 1931, first one-man exhibition,
Museum Folkwang, Essen.

STANDING FIGURE (STEHENDE FIGUR). 1966.
Carrara Marble, H. 79″.
Lent by the artist.
Carved directly in stone by the artist.

**GEORGE RICKEY**

Born 1907, South Bend, Indiana.
Residence East Chatham, New York.

1913, moved to Scotland. Education: 1921-26, attended Trinity College, Glenalmond, Scotland; 1926-29, Balliol College, Oxford, B.A.; 1928-29, Ruskin School of Drawing, Oxford; 1929-30, Académie André Lhote and Académie Moderne, Paris. 1945-46, Institute of Fine Arts, New York University, graduate study in the History of Art; 1947, State University of Iowa, studied etching under Maurice Lasansky; 1948-49, studied Institute of Design, Chicago. Travels: 1928-30, 1934, Germany; 1933-34, Paris; 1934-37, New York; 1939,

1940, 1951, 1959, Mexico. 1933, first one-man exhibition Caz-Delbo Gallery, New York. Awards: 1960, Guggenheim Foundation Fellowship (renewed 1961).

SIX LINES IN A T. 1965-66.
Stainless steel. H. 78½ x W. 128 x D. 30½".
Lent by Storm King Art Center, Mountainville, New York.
Constructed by the artist from preliminary drawings followed by experiments to arrive at proper balance and clearance for each bar.

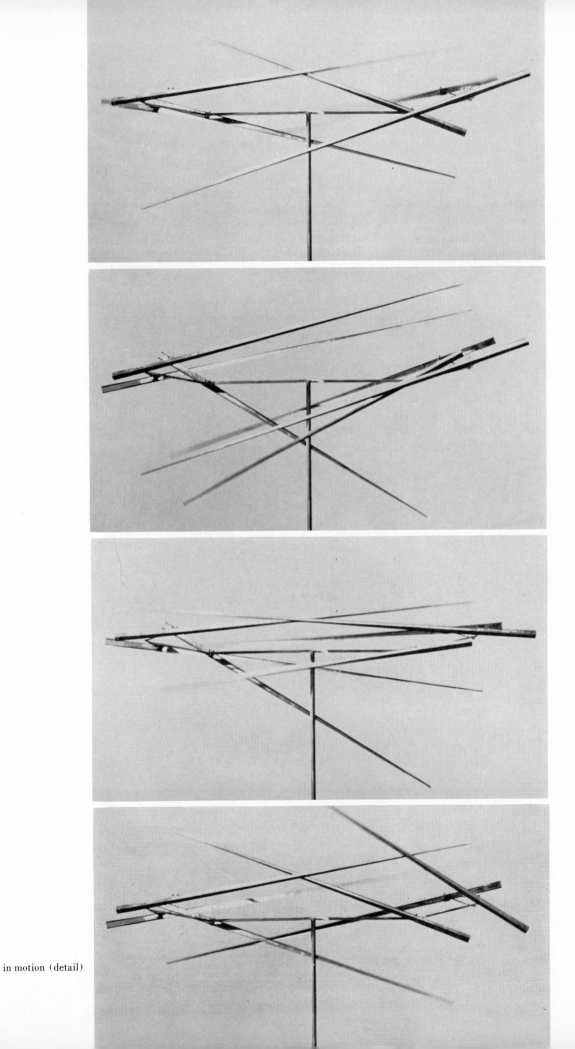

in motion (detail)

**MAX BILL**

Born 1908, Winterthur, Switzerland.
Residence Zurich.

Education: 1924-27, Kunstgewerbeschule, Zurich (trained as silver-smith) ; 1927-29, Bauhaus, Hochschule für Gestaltung, Dessau. 1953, lectured Colorado, Rio de Janeiro, São Paulo, and Paris; 1958, lectured Stuttgart, Hamburg, Hilversum. 1963, visited Canada. Active as architect, sculptor, painter and industrial designer. 1945, first one-man exhibition, Galerie des Eaux-Vives, Zurich. Awards: 1936 and 1951, Grand Prix for the design of the Swiss Pavillion, Milan Triennale; 1949, Kandinsky Prize; 1951, First International Sculpture Prize, I São Paulo Bienal.

UNIT OF THREE EQUAL VOLUMES. 1965.
Black granite, H. 31″.
Lent by Storm King Art Center, Mountainville, New York.
Made after the artist's designs and specifications by professional stone masons.

**GIACOMO MANZÙ**

Born 1908, Bergamo, Italy.
Residence Ardea, Rome.

Education: attended evening classes at at the Accademia Ciognini, Milan. 1930, moved to Milan; 1936, Paris. 1937, first one-man exhibition, Galleria Cometa, Rome. 1949, commission for doors of St. Peter's, Rome. 1957, commission for doors of Salzburg Cathedral. Awards: 1948, Prize for Italian Sculpture, XXIV Venice Biennale; 1965, Lenin Peace Prize.

SKATER (PATTINATRICE). 1958-66.
Wood, H. 63½″.
Collection Algur H. Meadows, Dallas.
Carved directly by the artist.

# III

| | |
|---|---|
| SERRANO | R. MÜLLER |
| HORIUTI | NEGRET |
| COUZIJN | CÉSAR |
| JACOBSEN | D'HAESE |
| A. SMITH | TOVISH |
| AGOSTINI | BURY |
| ÉTIENNE-MARTIN | STANKIEWICZ |
| ARMITAGE | TURNBULL |
| HOFLEHNER | KELLY |
| V. RICHTER | CARO |
| BLADEN | CHILLIDA |
| JARNUSZKIEWICZ | HAESE |
| CASCELLA | MALICH |
| CONSAGRA | PAOLOZZI |
| IPOUSTEGUY | |

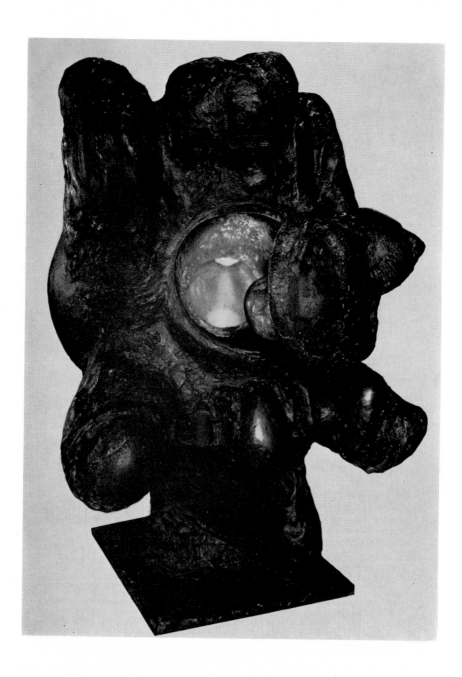

**PABLO SERRANO**

Born 1910, Crivillén-Teruel, Spain.
Residence Madrid.

Education: 1922, Barcelona. 1930, moved to Montevideo, Uruguay; 1956, travelled through Europe; 1957, Italy. 1956, first one-man exhibition, Ateneo de Madrid, Sala Santa Catalina. Awards: 1955, Grand Prize, Second Biennale, Montevideo; 1955, Grand Prize, Third Biennale Hispanoamericana, Barcelona; 1961, "Julio González" Prize, Critics Prize, Salon de Mayo, Barcelona.

MAN WITH A DOOR. 1965.
Bronze, H. 54½″.
Lent by the Galeriá Juana Mordó, Madrid.
Cast by the lost wax process in an edition of one bronze only.

**MASAKAZU HORIUTI**

Born 1911, Kyoto.
Residence Tokyo.

Education: School of Applied Arts, Tokyo; Municipal University of
Fine Arts, Kyoto (studied with Yuzo Figikawa). Professor, Kyoto
Municipal University of Fine Arts. 1963, first one-man exhibition,
Kamakura Museum of Modern Art. 1963, Kotaro Takano Prize.

HEXAHEDRON WITH DIMPLES. 1967.
Bronze, H. 21¼".
Lent by Kyoto Municipal Museum of Art.
Cast by the lost wax method in an edition of **three bronzes from the**
artist's original plaster.

**WESSEL COUZIJN**

Born 1912, Amsterdam.
Residence Amsterdam.

Education: 1929-30, Art Students League, New York; 1930-31, Rijksakademie, Amsterdam (studied with Professor J. Bonner). Went to Paris before World War II; 1940-45, worked in United States. 1959, first one-man exhibition, Rotterdamsche Kunstkring, Rotterdam. Awards: 1936, Prix de Rome; 1951, First Prize for Benelux countries for Monument to Political Prisoners; 1955, Nederlandsee Staatsprijs voor Beeldhouwkunst; 1965, Burgemeester van Grunsvenprijs, Heerlen; 1966, David Röellprijs.

SEATED GREEK (ZITTENDE GRIEK). 1964-65.
Bronze, H. 50″.
Lent by the artist.
Cast by the raw sand process from the artist's original plaster.

**ROBERT JACOBSEN**

Born 1912, Copenhagen.
Residence Paris.

Self taught. 1947, moved to Paris. 1944, first one-man exhibition, Galerie T. H. Hansen, Copenhagen. Awards: Prix du Général Kofoed, Denmark; 1952, Prix d'Honneur du Journal Politiken, Copenhagen; 1966, First Prize for sculpture, XXXIII Venice Biennale.

POLYCHROMED SCULPTURE. 1960.
Iron, polychromed, H. 92½ x W. 42½ x D. 30″.
Lent by Galerie Chalette, New York.
Welded assemblage.

**ANTHONY SMITH**

Born 1912, South Orange, New Jersey.
Residence South Orange, New Jersey.

Education: 1931-35, attended Art Students League, New York; 1937-38, attended New Bauhaus, Chicago, (studied with Moholy Nagy, Archipenko, and Kepes) ; 1939-40, studied architecture with Frank Lloyd Wright. 1953-55, lived in Germany. 1940-60, practicing architect.

BLACK BOX. 1962.
Steel, H. 22½ x W. 33 x D. 25″.
Lent by Fischbach Gallery, New York.
Made to the artist's specifications by an industrial fabricator.

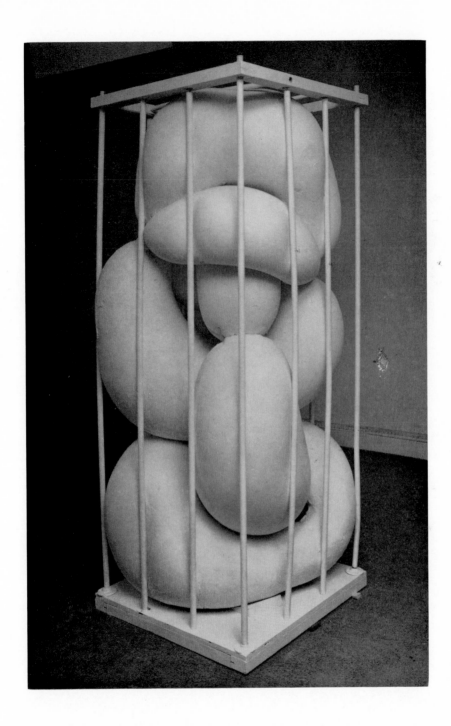

**PETER AGOSTINI**

Born 1913, New York.
Residence New York.

Education: Leonardo da Vinci Art School, New York. 1959, first one-
man exhibition, Galerie Grimaud, New York. Awards: 1960, 1961,
1962, Longview Foundation Grant; 1964, Brandeis University Creative Arts Award for Sculpture.

CAGE II. 1967.
Plaster, wood and steel, H. 76″.
Lent by Stephen Radich Gallery, New York.
Cast in plaster using pneumatic rubber inner tubes as forms.

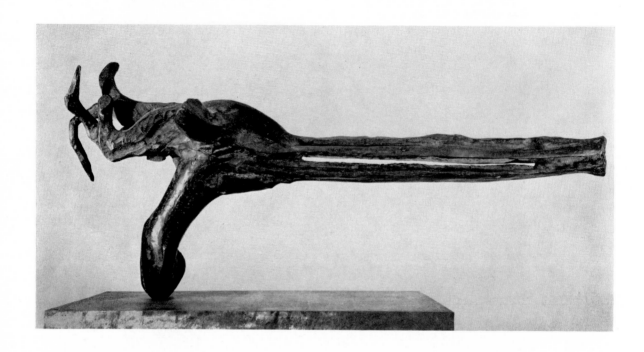

**ÉTIENNE-MARTIN**

Born 1913, Loriol (Drôme), France.
Residence Paris.

Education: 1929-33, École des Beaux-Arts, Lyons; 1933, Académie Ranson, Paris (studied with Maffray). 1960, first one-man exhibition, Galerie Breteau, Paris. Awards: 1938, Prix Paris-Lyon; 1948, Prix Blumenthal; 1949, Prix de la Jeune Sculpture; 1963, Copley Foundation Grant; 1966, Grand Sculpture Prize, XXXIII Venice Biennale.

THE BEAK (LE BEC). 1964.
Bronze, H. 26¼ x W. 58½ x D. 26".
Lent by Lefebre Gallery, New York.
Cast by the lost wax process in an edition of nine bronzes, of which this is the first, from the original wooden maquette carved directly by the artist.

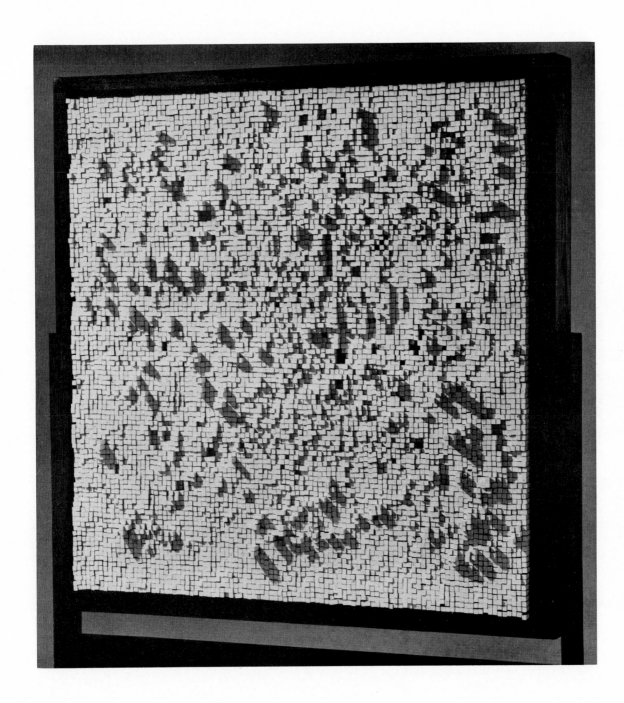

**VJENCESLAV RICHTER**

Born 1917, Zagreb, Yugoslavia.
Residence, Zagreb.

Education: 1949, Faculté de Technique de Zagreb, (studied architecture). 1936-63, travelled in Germany, Hungary, Austria, Czechoslovakia, Sweden, Switzerland, United States, England, France, Syria, Belgium, Holland, U.S.S.R. 1956, first one-man exhibition, Art Pavilion, Belgrade.

RELIEF METER (RELIEFOMÈTRE). 1964-67.
Plastic, steel, wood, H. 72 x W. 43 x D. 7″.
Lent by the artist.
Based on an earlier and slightly smaller work made in plastic under the artist's supervision, this structure was built in a factory in two almost identical versions to Richter's exact specifications.

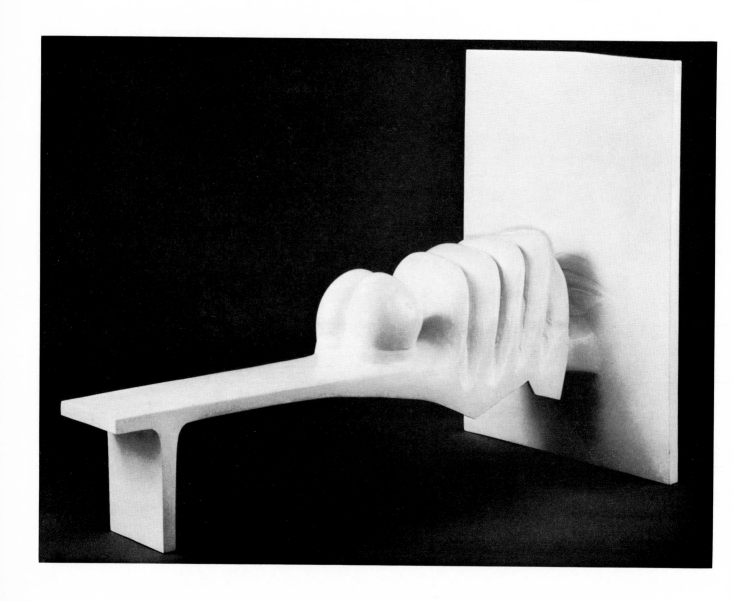

**KENNETH ARMITAGE**

Born 1916, Leeds, Yorkshire, England.
Residence, London.

Education: Leeds College of Art; 1937-39, Slade School, London.
1946-56, head of Sculpture Department, Bath Academy of Art. 1952,
first one-man exhibition, Gimpel Fils, London. Awards: 1953-55,
Gregory Fellowship in Sculpture, Leeds University; 1958, "David
E. Bright Foundation Award for the Best Sculptor under 45," XXIX
Venice Biennale.

THE BED. 1965.
Polyester resin, glass fiber reinforced, H. 48½ x W. 35½ x D. 68½".
Lent by the artist.
Cast in polyester from the artist's orginal plaster model.

**RUDOLF HOFLEHNER**

Born 1916, Linz, Austria.
Residence Stuttgart and Vienna.

Education: 1932-36, Staatsgewerbeschule für Maschinenbau, Linz;
1936-38, Technische Hochschule, Graz, Austria (studied architecture) ; 1938-40, Akademie der Bildenden Künste, Vienna. 1951-54,
worked with Wotruba. 1965, visited New York. 1951, first one-man
exhibition, Neue Galerie der Stadt Linz, Austria, and Galerie d' Art
Moderne, Basel. 1959, Prize of the City of Vienna.

FIGURE 101: THE COUPLE. 1966.
Steel (unicat), H. 43 x W. 79 x D. 16″.
Lent by the artist.
Chiseled and polished by the artist from solid steel.

**RONALD BLADEN**

Born 1918, Vancouver, British Columbia.
Residence New York.

Education: 1936-37, Vancouver School of Art; 1939, California
School of Fine Arts, San Francisco. 1955, first one-man exhibition,
University of British Columbia (painting). Awards: Rosenberg
Fellowship; San Francisco Art Association; National Arts Council.

BLACK TRIANGLE. 1966.
Painted wood, (to be made in metal), H. 112 x W. 141 x D. 120".
Lent by Fischbach Gallery, New York.

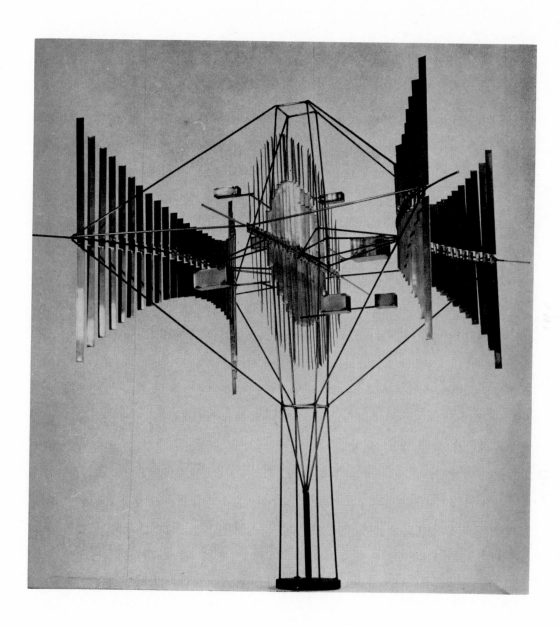

**JERZY JARNUSZKIEWICZ**

Born 1919, Kalisz, Poland.
Residence Warsaw.

Education: 1950, Academy of Fine Arts, Department of Sculpture, Warsaw. 1950, travelled in Switzerland, France, Belgium, Austria, U.S.S.R.; 1957, Austria, Czechoslovakia, Switzerland, Italy; 1959, France; 1964, Yugoslavia. 1964, first one-man exhibition, Ravne, Yugoslavia. Awards: First Class State Prize, Poland; 1966, team prize, International Competition for the Auschwitz Monument.

RHYTHMS II. 1965-1966.
Stainless steel, H. 44½ x W. 35 x D. 42½".
Lent by the artist.
Welded assemblage.

**ANDREA CASCELLA**

Born 1920, Pescara.
Residence Milan.

Education: trained by his father, Tommaso Cascella. Executed ceramic architectural decoration in Rome. 1949, first one-man exhibition, Galleria dell'Obelisco, Rome. Awards: 1958, winner with his brother of International competition for Auschwitz Monument; 1964, First Prize for Sculpture, XXXII Venice Biennale.

NARCISSUS (NARCISO). 1967.
Black Belgian marble, H. 36″.
Lent by Galleria dell 'Ariete, Milan.
Direct carving.

**PIETRO CONSAGRA**

Born 1920, Mazara del Vallo, Sicily.
Residence Rome.

Education: 1938-44, Academy of Fine Arts, Palermo. 1946, visited
Paris. 1946-47, one of the founders of abstract group, *Forma*, in
Rome. 1947, first one-man exhibition, Galleria Mola, Rome. Awards:
1955, Metallurgica Prize, III São Paulo Bienal; 1956, Einaudi Prize,
XXVIII Venice Biennale; 1958, Honorable Mention, Pittsburgh International and Belgian Art Critics' Prize, World's Fair, Brussels; 1959, First Prize, II Morgan's Paint, Rimini; 1960, Grand Prize
for Sculpture, XXX Venice Biennale.

TURQUOISE IRON (FERRO TURCHESE). 1966.
Painted iron, H. 99".
Lent by Marlborough Galleria d'Arte, Rome.

80

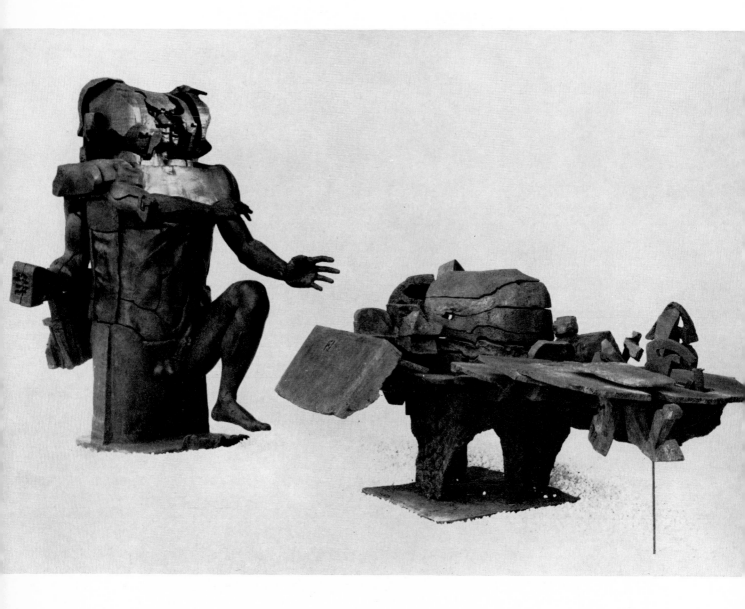

**JEAN IPOUSTEGUY**

Born 1920, Dun-sur-Meuse, France.
Residence Paris.

Education: 1938, worked with Robert Lesbounit, Paris. 1954, first
one-man exhibition, Galerie de Beaune, Paris. Awards: 1964, "David
E. Bright Foundation Award for the Best Sculptor under 45,",
XXXII Venice Biennale.

ALEXANDER BEFORE ECBATANA
(ALEXANDRE DEVANT ECBATANE). 1965.
Bronze, H. 68 x W. 47¼ x D. 158".
Lent by Galerie Claude Bernard, Paris.
Cast in separate parts by the lost expandable polystyrene process in
an edition of six bronzes. Ecbatana, capitol of the Near Eastern
empire of Medea, was conquered and plundered by Alexander the
Great in 330 B.C.

Detail

**ROBERT MÜLLER**

Born 1920, Zurich.
Residence Villiers-le-Bel, near Paris.

Education: 1939-44, pupil of Charles Otto Bänninger and Germaine
Richier. 1947-50, Italy. 1950, moved to Paris. 1954, first one-man
exhibition, Galerie Craven, Paris.

ORGAN (L'ORGUE). 1966.
Iron, H. 83″.
Collection Stedelijk Museum, Amsterdam.
Welded assemblage.

**EDGAR NEGRET**

Born 1920, Popayan, Colombia.
Residence Bogotá, Colombia.

Education: School of Fine Arts, Cali, Colombia. Worked with Jorge Oteira in Popayan and Madrid. 1949, United States, studied metal work at New York Sculpture Center. 1951-55, travelled in Europe (Paris and Madrid). 1943, first one-man exhibition, Conservatoire de Cali. 1958, grant from UNESCO to study Indian art in North America.

TOWER NO. 2. 1965-66.
Aluminum polychromed, H. 83".
Lent by the Graham Gallery, New York.
Bolted aluminum sheets cut and assembled by the artist.

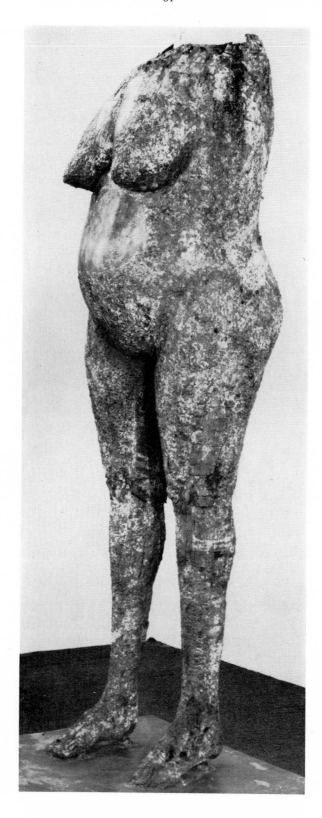

**CÉSAR (BALDACCINI)**

Born 1921, Marseille.
Residence Paris.

Education: 1935-39, École des Beaux Arts de Marseille; 1943, École des Beaux-Arts, Paris. 1954, first one-man exhibition, Galerie Durand, Paris. 1957, First Prize for Foreign Participation, Biennale de Carrara, Italy.

THE VICTORY OF VILLETANEUSE
(LA VICTOIRE DE VILLETANEUSE). 1965.
Iron, H. 88½".
Lent by Galerie Claude Bernard, Paris.
Welded assemblage, subsequently braised and polished irregularly by the artist. From this original iron version an edition of nine bronzes has been cast.

**ROËL D'HAESE**

Born 1921, Grammont, Belgium.
Residence Nieuport-Bains, Belgium.

Education: 1932, Académie d'Alost, Belgium; 1938-42, École Nationale Supérieure d'Architecture et des Arts Décoratifs, Brussels (worked with sculptor, Oscar Jaspers). 1949, first one-man exhibition, Galerie Lou Cousyn, Brussels. Awards: 1954, Prize for a Young Belgian sculptor, René Lust Foundation; 1958, Belgian Critics Prize; 1960, Prix de l'Académie Picard.

THE HAPPY VIOLIN. 1965.
Bronze, H. 55″.
Lent by Galerie van de Loo, Munich.
Cast in bronze by the lost wax method.

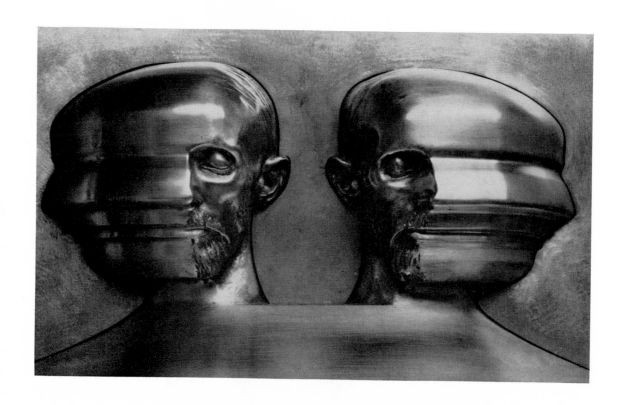

**HAROLD TOVISH**

Born 1921, New York.
Residence Brookline, Massachusetts.

Education: 1938-40, W.P.A. Art School, New York; 1940-43, Columbia University, New York; 1949-50, Ossip Zadkine School of Sculpture, Paris; 1950-51, Académie de la Grande Chaumière, Paris. 1949-51, Paris; 1954-57, Florence; 1965-66, Rome. 1954, first one-man exhibition, Walker Art Center, Minneapolis. Awards: 1951, Purchase Prize, Walker Art Center; 1952-54, First Prize, Minneapolis Art Institute; 1957, Honorable Mention, Portland Society of Art; 1957-59, First Prize, Sculpture, Boston Arts Festival; 1958, First Prize, Drawing, Boston Arts Festival; 1959, Margaret Brown Award, Institute of Contemporary Art, Boston; 1960, Grant, American Institute of Arts and Letters; 1964, Second Prize, Sculpture, Boston Arts Festival.

PASSAGE. 1964-65.     (Illustration shows a detail.)
Bronze, H. 40″.
Joseph H. Hirshhorn Collection.

**POL BURY**

Born 1922, Haine-St.-Pierre, Belgium.
Residence Saulx-les-Chartreux, France, and New York.

Education: 1935, Athenée Provincial du Centre, La Louvière, Belgium; 1938-39 Académie des Beaux-Arts, Mons. Travelled in Italy, United States. 1945, first one-man exhibition, Galerie Lou Cousyn, Brussels (painting); 1953, first one-man exhibition, Galerie Apollo, Brussels (sculpture). 1964, Prix Selection Marzotto.

INCLINED PLANE WITH FORTY-NINE SPHERES. 1966.
Wood polychromed with motorized elements, H. 71 x W. 23¾ x D. 44½".
Lent by Lefebre Gallery, New York.
Constructed by the artist.

**RICHARD STANKIEWICZ**

Born 1922, Philadelphia.
Residence Huntington, Massachusetts.

Education: 1948-49, Hofmann School with Hans Hofmann; 1950-51, Atelier Fernand Léger, Paris; 1950-51, Zadkine School of Sculpture, Paris. Travelled Europe, United States. 1953, first one-man exhibition, Hansa Gallery, New York.

WIND GONG II. 1967.
Steel, H. 59".
Lent by the artist.
Welded assemblage.

**WILLIAM TURNBULL**

Born 1922, Dundee, Scotland.
Residence London.

Education: 1947-48, Slade School of Art, London. 1948-50, lived in
Paris. 1957, first visit to United States. 1962, travelled in Japan, Cam-
bodia, and Malaysia. 1950, first one-man exhibition, Hanover Gallery,
London.

3X1, SECOND VERSION. 1966.
Painted steel, H. 84½ x W. 93 x D. 31″.
Lent by the artist.
Made to the artist's specifications by an industrial fabricator.

**ELLSWORTH KELLY**

Born 1923, Newburgh, New York.
Residence New York.

Education: 1946-48, Boston Museum School; 1948, Académie des Beaux-Arts, Paris. 1948-54, travelled in France. 1951, first one-man exhibition, Galerie Arnaud, Paris. Awards: 1961, Carnegie Award, Pittsburgh International Exhibition; 1962, Brandeis University Creative Arts Award; 1963, Mainichi Prize, Tokyo Biennale.

RED—BLUE ROCKER. 1963.
Aluminum, polychromed, H. 72½″.
Lent by Robert Fraser Gallery, London.
Executed by the artist from drawings and maquettes.

**ANTHONY CARO**

Born 1924, London.
Residence London.

Education: 1942, Christ's College, Cambridge (studied engineering); 1946, Regent Street Polytechnic (studied sculpture); 1947-52, Royal Academy Schools, London. 1951-53, Assistant to Henry Moore. 1956, first one-man exhibition, Galleria del Naviglio, Milan. 1963-65, taught at Bennington College, Vermont.

MIDDAY. 1960.
Painted steel, H. 94 x W. 38 x D. 150″.
Collection Timothy and Paul Caro, London.
Welded and bolted assemblage.

### EDUARDO CHILLIDA

Born 1924, San Sebastian, Spain.
Residence San Sebastian and Paris.

Education: 1943-47, studied architecture, Madrid. 1948-51, Paris. 1954, first one-man exhibition, Galerie Clan, Madrid. Awards: 1958, Graham Foundation, Chicago; 1958, Grand Prize for Sculpture, XXIX Venice Biennale; 1960, Kandinsky Prize; 1964, Carnegie Award, Pittsburgh International Exhibition; 1966, Wilhelm Lehmbruck Prize of the City of Duisberg; 1966, Nordrhein-Westfalen Prize, Düsseldorf.

SPACE MODULATION IV
(MODULATION DE L'ESPACE IV). 1966.
Iron, H. 22¾ x W. 41¼ x D. 37¾".
Collection Aimé Maeght, Paris.
Forged by the artist from rectangular iron bars.

**GÜNTER HAESE**

Born 1924, Kiel, Germany.
Residence Düsseldorf.

Education: 1948-49, Kunstschule auf dem Steinberg, Plön Hol-
stein, Germany; 1950-57, Düsseldorf Academy (studied with Bruno
Goller and Edward Mataré). 1964, first one-man exhibition, Ulm
Museum, Ulm, Germany.

OLYMP. 1967.
Brass, copper, H. 36⅝ x W. 29¾ x D. 23⅛".
Lent by the artist.
Braised and soldered assemblage of found objects and components
pre-formed by the artist.

**KAREL MALICH**

Born 1924, Holice, Bohemia.
Residence Prague.

Education: 1945-49, Karlova Universita, Prague (studied drawing);
1950-55, Akademie Výtvarného Umĕni, Prague (studied graphics).
Travelled U.S.S.R., Poland, Yugoslavia, France and Italy. Member
of *Promena* and *Umĕlecká beseda* groups. 1946, first one-man exhibition, Prague.

BLACK AND WHITE SCULPTURE. 1964-65.
Plastic, wood and aluminum, H. 82½″.
Lent by the artist.

**EDUARDO PAOLOZZI**

Born 1924, Edinburgh.
Residence London.

Education: Edinburgh College of Art and Slade School of Fine Art, London. Travelled extensively in Europe and United States. 1947, first one-man exhibition, Mayor Gallery, London. Awards: 1953, British Critics Prize; 1960, "David E. Bright Foundation Award for Best Sculptor under 45," XXX Venice Biennale.

INVERSION (UMKEHRUNG). 1966.
Steel, chrome plated, H. 29¼ x W. 49¾ x D. 29¾".
Lent by Pace Gallery, New York.

# IV

| | |
|---|---|
| KOLÍBAL | MIYAWAKI |
| KRASINSKI | OLDENBURG |
| TINGUELY | YUHARA |
| PFAHLER | MORRIS |
| SEGAL | SHINODA |
| BEN-SCHMUEL | DI SUVERO |
| CHAMBERLAIN | LENK |
| KOWALSKI | KING |
| TROVA | MC CRACKEN |
| TRŠAR | TUCKER |
| JUDD | SAKAKI |
| YAMAGUCHI | MURRAY |
| LUGINBÜHL | BELL |
| MEADMORE | FUKUSHIMA |

**STANISLAV KOLÍBAL**

Born 1925, Orlov, Czechoslovakia.
Residence Prague.

Education: 1945-50, Applied Art School, Prague, (studied with Professor Antonín Strnadel) ; 1951-54, Art Academy, Prague, (studied stage design with Professor František Tröster). Member of group UB12. Travelled in Greece, Belgium, Egypt, Syria, Lebanon, Italy, Great Britain, France. 1960, first one-man exhibition, Aleš Hall, Prague.

THE TABLE. 1965.
Aluminum, H. 34 x W. 48 x D. 38″.
Lent by the artist.
Cast by the lost wax method from the original full-scale plaster.

**EDWARD KRASINSKI**

Born 1925, Tuck, Poland.
Residence Warsaw.

Education: 1945-50, Academy, Krakow. 1965, first one-man exhibition, Krysztofory Gallery, Krakow.

NO. 7, 1967. 1967.
Aluminum, plastic, wood, polychromed, H. 98½″.
Lent by the artist.

**JEAN TINGUELY**

Born 1925, Fribourg, Switzerland.
Residence Soisy-sur-Ecole, near Paris.

Education: 1941-45, École des Beaux-Arts, Basel. 1952, Paris; 1959, Stockholm, London; 1961, Figueras, (Spain), Copenhagen; 1960-66, visited New York periodically. 1954, first one-man exhibition, Galerie Arnaud, Paris.

ROTOZAZA, No. 1. 1967.
Iron, wood, motorized elements, H. 87 x W. 162 x D. 91".
Lent by Galerie Alexandre Iolas, Paris.

**GEORG KARL PFAHLER**

Born 1926, Emetzheim/Weissenburg, Bavaria.
Residence Stuttgart.

Education: 1950-54, Kunstakademie, Stuttgart. 1959, first one-man
exhibition, Galerie Rauls, Stuttgart. 1964, visited New York.
1957, Prize "der Jugend für Malerei".

COLOR SPACE OBJECT 13 (FARBRAUMOBJEKT 13). 1966-67.
Steel, polychromed (three pieces), H. 71 x W. 63 x D. 115½″.
Lent by Galerie Müller, Stuttgart.
Executed by an industrial fabricator from the artist's specifications
and original maquette.

**GEORGE SEGAL**

Born 1926, New York.
Residence North Brunswick, New Jersey.

Education: 1950, New York University, B.S.; 1963, Rutgers University, M.A.; 1956, first one-man exhibition, Hansa Gallery, New York. Awards: Walter K. Gutman Foundation Grant; 1966, Mr. and Mrs. Frank G. Logan Gold Medal, The Art Institute of Chicago.

THE BILL BOARD. 1966.  (left)
Plaster, wood, metal, rope, H. 189 x W. 117 x D. 20″.
Lent by Sidney Janis Gallery, New York.
The plaster figure was cast in sections directly from a life model.

**DAN BEN-SCHMUEL**

Born 1927, near Dublin.
Residence New York, since 1966.

Self-educated. Lived and worked in Ireland, Africa, South America, England, Europe and 1961-66, Israel. Became Israeli citizen.

ICONOGRAM. 1967.  (above)
Copper on wood base, H. 87 x W. 66½ x D. 69½″.
Lent by the artist.
Braised, soldered, and welded assemblage.

**JOHN CHAMBERLAIN**

Born 1927, Rochester, Indiana.
Residence New York.

Education: 1950-52, Chicago Art Institute School; 1955-56, Black Mountain College, North Carolina. 1957, first one-man exhibition, Wells Street Gallery, Chicago.

TUNG TING HU. 1967.
Flexible polyurethane, H. 37¼ x W. 54 x D. 51¾".
Lent by the artist.
The polyurethane was folded and tied with cords, following which the artist cut and shaped it with a knife.

**PIOTR KOWALSKI**

Born 1927, Warsaw.
Residence Paris.

1946, Brazil. Education: 1947-52, Harvard University, (studied architecture). 1952-53, New York; 1953-55, Paris. 1961, first one-man exhibition, Maison des Beaux-Arts, Paris. Awards: 1961, First Prize, Competition for the construction of a railway station, Tunis; 1962, Third Prize, competition for the international "Baumuseum," Paris; 1963, Graham Foundation for Advanced Studies in Fine Arts, Chicago.

CUBE V. 1967.
Steel and plaster, H. 35 x W. 35 x D. 35".
Lent by the artist.

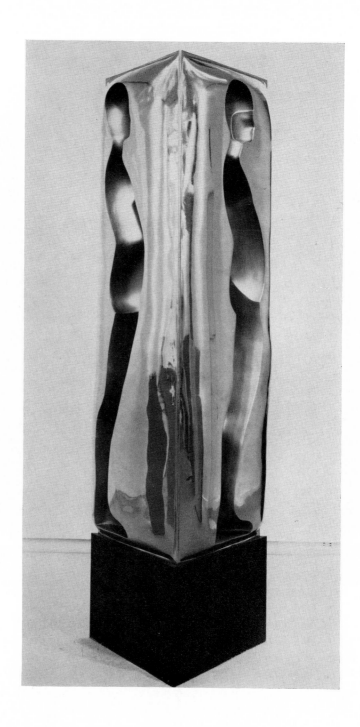

**ERNEST TROVA**

Born 1927, St. Louis.
Residence St. Louis.

Self-taught. 1959, first one-man exhibition, Image Gallery, St. Louis.

STUDY FALLING MAN: INTAGLIO. 1966.
Polished bronze. H. 78½″.
Collection Mr. and Mrs. David L. Paul, New York.
Each of the vertical side panels was cast by the lost wax method from
a plaster model, following which the panels were welded together.

**DONALD JUDD**

Born 1928, Excelsior Springs, Missouri.
Residence New York.

Education: 1947-53, Art Student's League, New York; 1948-49, College of William and Mary, Williamsburg, Virginia; 1953, Columbia University, B.S.; 1958-61, Fine Arts Department, Columbia University. 1963-64, first one-man exhibition, Green Gallery, New York.

UNTITLED (EIGHT MODULAR UNIT V-CHANNEL PIECE). 1966.
Painted steel, H. 48¼ x W. 125⅝ x D. 127½″ (in 8 sections).
Lent by Ferus Gallery, Los Angeles.
Made to the artist's specifications by an industrial fabricator.

**DRAGO TRŠAR**

Born 1927, Planina-Koper, Yugoslavia.
Residence Ljubljana, Yugoslavia.

Education: Academy of Fine Arts, Ljubljana. Travelled in Italy, France, Belgium, Egypt, Austria. 1960, first one-man exhibition, Mala Gallery, Ljubljana. Awards: 1955, Sculpture Prize, Mediterranean Biennale, Alexandria; 1961, Sculpture Prize, Triennale, Belgrade; 1961, Medal, III Morgan's Paint, Rimini.

THE CHANNEL (KANAL). 1966.
Bronze, H. 23¼ x W. 24 x D. 15″.
Lent by the artist, courtesy Adria Art Gallery, New York.
Cast by the lost wax method from a plaster based on the original clay model.

**KATSUHIRO YAMAGUCHI**

Born 1928, Tokyo.
Residence Tokyo.

Education: 1949-52, Nihon University, Tokyo (studied law). 1961-62, travelled in Italy, Spain, New York. 1952, first one-man exhibition, Matsushima Gallery, Tokyo.

THE PORT. 1966.
Acrylic plastic, electric lights, H. 63".
Lent by the artist, courtesy Minami Gallery, Tokyo.
Made by the artist in collaboration with an industrial fabricator.

**CLEMENT MEADMORE**

Born 1929, Melbourne, Australia.
Residence New York, since 1963.

Education: Royal Melbourne Technical College (studied industrial design and engineering). 1953, travelled in Europe. 1959, Japan. 1954, first one-man exhibition, Melbourne.

TURN-UP. 1966.
Polystyrene, H. 51 x W. 53¾ x D. 53¾″.
Lent by the artist.
Fabricated by the artist, based on a small-scale maquette.

**AIKO MIYAWAKI**

Born 1929, Tokyo.
Residence Tokyo.

Education: 1952, graduated from the Japan Women's University, Tokyo; 1958, Bunka Gakuin, Tokyo (studied painting with Nebuya Abe and Yeshishige Saito); 1957, Santa Monica City College and University of California, Los Angeles. Since 1957, travelled in the United States, Mexico, India, Turkey and Europe. 1959, first one-man exhibition, Yoseido Gallery, Tokyo.

WORK BRASS 402- No. 15, SERIES A. 1966.
Brass, wood, H. 46 x W. 46 x D. 7".
Lent by Tokyo Gallery, Tokyo.
Made to the artist's specifications by an industrial fabricator.

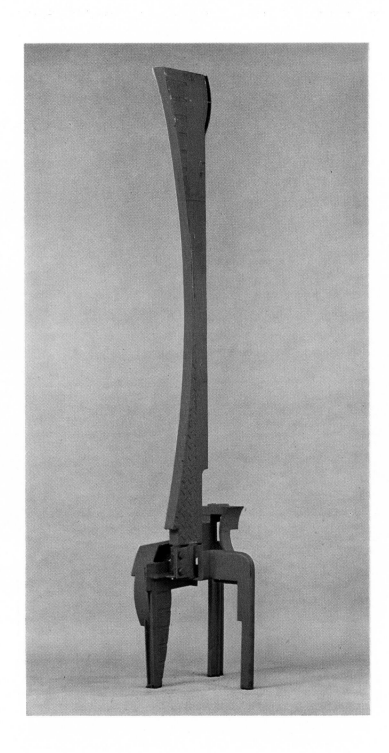

**BERNARD LUGINBÜHL**

Born 1929, Bern, Switzerland.
Residence Mötschwil, near Bern.

Education: 1945-48, sculptor apprenticeship; École des Arts et Métiers, Bern. 1949, studio in Bern; 1951, studio in Moôsseedorf, near Bern. 1961, first one-man exhibition, Galerie Renée Ziegler, Zurich.

LITTLE GIRAFFE (KLEINE GIRAFFE). 1965.
Painted iron, H. 97½".
Lent by Galerie Renée Ziegler, Zurich, Switzerland.

113

### CLAES OLDENBURG

Born 1929, Stockholm.
Residence New York.

Raised in Chicago. Education: 1950, Yale University, B.A.; 1952-55, Chicago Art Institute School (studied with Paul Wieghardt). Travelled in United States, Europe. 1950-52, apprentice reporter. Operated the Ray Gun Manufacturing Company, New York. 1959, first one-man exhibition, Judson Gallery, New York.

GIANT SOFT DRUM SET. 1967.
Canvas, vinyl, wood, H. c. 84″.
Lent by Sidney Janis Gallery, New York.
Stitched and sewn together by the artist from materials cut to patterns based on preliminary drawings and a small scale model.
(Illustration is of a preliminary drawing.)

**KAZUO YUHARA**

Born 1930, Tokyo.
Residence Yokahama.

Education: 1951-58, University of Fine Arts, Tokyo; 1955-57, University of Tokyo (graduate studies in sculpture). 1963, travelled in Paris, Italy and Spain. Awards: 1958, First Prize for sculpture by a young artist, Annual Exhibition of Japanese Art, Municipal Museum, Tokyo; 1963, First Prize Maruzen-Sekiyu Bijutsu-Shôreishô Competition.

NO. 1. 1966.
Steel, chrome plated, H. 26″.
Collection Richard Brown Baker, New York.
Made to the artist's specifications by an industrial fabricator.

**ROBERT MORRIS**

Born 1931, Kansas City, Missouri.
Residence New York.

Education: 1948-50, University of Kansas City and Kansas City Art
Institute; 1951, California School of Fine Arts, San Francisco; 1954-
55, Reed College, Portland, Oregon; 1961-62, graduate work in Art
History, Hunter College, New York. 1957, first one-man exhibition,
Dilexi Gallery, San Francisco.

UNTITLED. 1967.
Steel, H. 36 x W. 180 x D. 180″ (9 units, each 36 x 36 x 36″).
Lent by Leo Castelli Gallery, New York.
Made to the artist's specifications by an industrial fabricator.

**MORIO SHINODA**

Born 1931, Tokyo.
Residence Houston, Texas.

Education: 1949-52, Aoyama Gakuin University; 1963-64, The Art
Institute of Chicago. 1967, first one-man exhibition, Kiko Galleries,
Houston. Awards: 1956, Prize, Modern Art Exhibition, Japan; 1965,
Museum prize, Museum of Modern Art, Kamakura, Ube City; 1966,
Kotaro Takamura Sculpture Prize.

TENSION AND COMPRESSION, NO. 345. 1966.
Cast iron, chrome plated, H. 56″.
Collection Kenneth Schnitzer, Houston, Texas.
The suspended segment was cast in iron by the raw sand process
from the original plaster; the iron base was fabricated industrially
to the artist's specifications.

**MARK DI SUVERO**

Born 1933, Shanghai, China.
Residence New York.

1941, came to the United States. Education: University of California,
B.A. Travelled in the United States and Mexico. 1960, first one-man
exhibition, Green Gallery, New York. Awards: Longview Foundation Grant; 1963, jury award, 66th American Painting and Sculpture
Annual, The Art Institute of Chicago.

SLICED BOILERMAKER. 1966-67.
Steel, H. 78 x W. 83 x D. 54".
Lent by Park Place Gallery, New York.
Cut, bolted, and welded assemblage.

**KASPAR-THOMAS LENK**

Born 1933, Berlin.
Residence Stuttgart.

Education: 1950, Kunstakademie, Stuttgart. 1967, visited New York.
1959, first one-man exhibition, Galerie Boukes, Wiesbaden.

STRATIFICATION 21a (SCHICHTUNG 21a). 1964-67.
Plexiglass, H. 83½ x W. 61¾ x D. 16¾".
Lent by Galerie Müller, Stuttgart.
Fabricated by the artist, based on a small-scale maquette.

**PHILIP KING**

Born 1934, Tunis, North Africa.
Residence London.

1945, moved to England. Education: 1954-57, Cambridge University
(modern languages) ; 1957, St. Martin's School of Art (studied with
Anthony Caro). 1958-59, assistant to Henry Moore. 1964, first one-
man exhibition, Heffers Gallery, Cambridge. 1959-60, Boise Scholar-
ship to Greece for three months.

BRAKE. 1966.
Fibreglass and plastic, H. 84 x W. 144 x D. 108″.
Lent by Rowan Gallery, London.
Made by an industrial fabricator in an edition of three from the
artist's full scale model.

**JOHN MC CRACKEN**

Born 1934, Berkeley, California.
Residence Venice, California.

Education: California College of Arts and Crafts. 1965, first one-man
exhibition, Nicholas Wilder Gallery, Los Angeles.

LOVE IN ITALIAN. 1967.
Plywood and fibreglass, H. 84½ x W. 48¼ x D. 2¾″.
Lent by Nicholas Wilder Gallery, Los Angeles.
A hollow wooden plank was constructed by the artist, coated with
fibreglass and sanded to a smooth surface, and then painted and
polished.

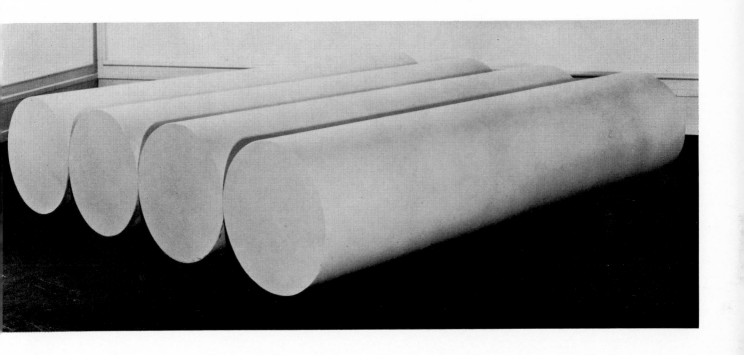

**WILLIAM TUCKER**

Born 1935, Cairo.
Residence London.

1937, went to England. Education: 1955-58, Oxford University (read history); 1958, St. Martin's and Central School of Art (studied sculpture). 1963, one-man exhibition, Rowan Gallery, London.

FOUR PART SCULPTURE NO. 1. 1966.
Fibreglass, H. 18 x W. 72 x D. 90".
Lent by the artist.
Following a concept previously decided upon, the artist painted a set of cylinders fabricated industrially to his specifications.

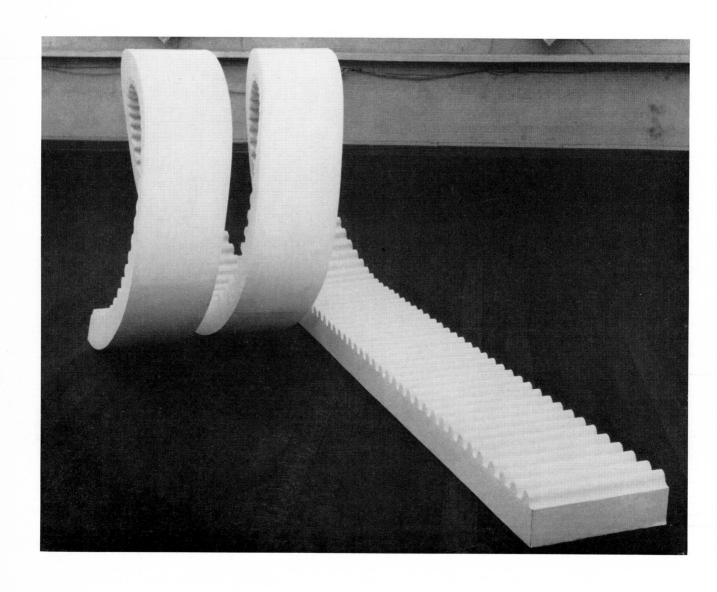

**KEN SAKAKI**

Born 1936, Osaka.
Residence Kyoto.

Education: 1959, graduated from Kyoto Municipal Art College. 1962,
first one-man exhibition, Galerie 16, Kyoto.

OPUS 66-10-7. 1966.
Wood, fabric, coated with plastic, H. 35¼ x W. 39½ x D. 89".
Lent by the artist, courtesy Galerie 16, Kyoto.
Constructed by the artist.

**NORIYASU FUKUSHIMA**

Born 1940, Tottori Prefecture, Kyoto.
Residence Kyoto.

Education: 1962, graduated from Kyoto Municipal Art College. 1964-65, visited the United States for 1½ years. 1964, assistant to Noguchi.

BLUE DOTS. 1966.
Wood and plastic polychromed, H. 52¼ x W. 126¼ x D. 43¼".
Lent by the artist, courtesy Galerie 16, Kyoto.
Fabricated by the artist.

**ROBERT MURRAY**

Born 1938, Vancouver, B.C.
Residence New York.

Education: 1956-58, School of Art, Regina College, University of
Saskatchewan; 1958-59, Instituto Allende, San Miguel, Mexico;
Artist's Workshops, Emma Lake, Saskatchewan (with Barnett New-
man, Will Barnet, John Ferren, and Clement Greenberg); 1960,
moved to New York City, attended Art Student's League. 1965, first
one-man exhibition, Betty Parsons Gallery, New York. 1960, Canada
Council Grant for Study in New York.

WINDFALL. 1966.
Aluminum polychromed, H. 48 x W. 114 x D. 24″.
Lent by Betty Parsons Gallery, New York.
Made in an industrial metalworks from the artist's drawings and
specifications.

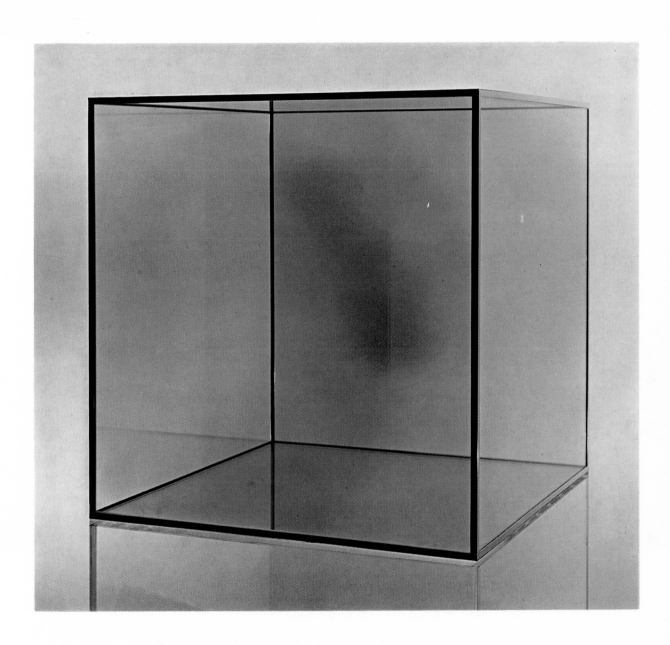

**LARRY BELL**

Born 1939, Chicago.
Residence New York and Venice, California.

Education: 1957-59, attended Chouinard Art Institute, Los Angeles.
1962, visited Mexico City. 1962, first one-man exhibition, Ferus Gallery, Los Angeles. 1963, William and Noma Copley Prize.

MEMORIES OF MIKE. 1967.
Vacuum plated glass, H. 24¼ x W. 24¼ x D. 24¼".
Collection Mr. and Mrs. Arnold B. Glimcher, New York.
Each of the six sides of the cube is flat optical glass that has been coated on the inner surface by means of a vacuum chamber process modified by the artist for his own use. After Bell completed the coating process, the glass sheets were assembled, cemented at their beveled edges, and secured with strips of chrome plated brass at the seams.

# BIBLIOGRAPHY

The bibliography refers to entries since 1960 and is organized in the following manner:

# I. GENERAL BIBLIOGRAPHY AND EXHIBITIONS

## A.

### BOOKS AND ARTICLES
(Arranged in chronological order)

GIEDION-WELCKER, CAROLA. *Contemporary Sculpture. An Evolution in Volume and Space*, New York, George Wittenborn, Inc., 1960. German edition, *Moderne Plastik*, Verlag Dr. H. Girsberger, Zurich, 1937; revised and enlarged English edition with bibliography by Bernard Karpel, no. 12 in the series "Documents of Modern Art", 1955.

JAGUER, EDOUARD. *Sculpture 1950-1960. Poétique de la sculpture*, Paris, La Musée de Poche, 1960.

SEUPHOR, MICHEL. *Sculpture of this Century*, New York, George Braziller, 1960. French edition, *La Sculpture de ce siècle, Dictionnaire de la sculpture moderne*, Neuchatel, Switzerland, Éditions du Griffon, 1959. German edition, Neuchatel, Switzerland, 1959.

*LA SCULPTURE CONTEMPORAINE*, 1900-1960, Paris, Éditions de l'Illustration, 1961. Vol. I, "La Sculpture française", text by Charles Kunstler; Vol. II, "La Sculpture étrangère", text by Cecile Goldscheider.

TRIER, EDOUARD. *Form and Space, Sculpture of the 20th Century*, New York, Frederick A. Praeger, 1961. Translated from the German by C. Ligota. German edition, *Figur und Raum. Die Skulptur des XX Jahrhunderts*, Berlin, Mann Verlag, 1960; English edition, London, Thames and Hudson, 1961.

LEBEL, ROBERT. *Anthologie des formes inventées. Un demi-siècle de sculpture*, Paris, Éditions de la Galerie du Cercle, 1962.

MAILLARD, ROBERT, ed. *A Dictionary of Modern Sculpture*, London, Methuen, 1962. French edition, *Dictionnaire de la sculpture moderne*, Paris, Fernand Hazen, 1960. German edition, *Knaurs Lexikon der Modernen Plastik*, Munich and Zurich, Dromersche Verlagsanstalt, 1961; translated from the French by Bettina Wadia.

VOLBOUDT, PIERRE. "Espace et Sculpture", *XX Siècle*, Paris, vol. 24, no. 18, February, 1962, pp. 3-12.

SELZ, JEAN. *Modern Sculpture, Origins and Evolution*, New York, George Braziller, 1963. Translated from the French by Annette Michelson. French edition, Lausanne, 1963; German edition, Munich, 1963.

ALLOWAY, LAWRENCE. "Sculpture as Cliché", *Artforum*, San Francisco, vol. II, no. 4, October, 1963, p. 26.

GERTZ, ULRICH. *Plastik der Gegenwart*. Berlin, Rembrandt Verlag, vol. 1, 1953; vol. 2, 1964.

GHEERBRANDT, BERNARD, and PARINAUD, ANDRÉ, eds. *Dictionnaire des Artistes contemporains: 50 artistes, peintres, sculpteurs, graveurs, présentés par 22 critiques en 1964*, Paris, Les Libraires Associés, 1964.

*Metro, International Directory of Contemporary Art, Catalogue International de l'Art Contemporain, Catalogo Internazionale dell'Arte Contemporanea*, Milan, Editoriale Metro, 1964.

BOUDAILLE, GEORGES. "Sculpture at the Crossroads", *Cimaise*, Paris, vol. 11, no. 68, April-June 3, 1964, pp. 47-59.

BOWNESS, ALAN. *Modern Sculpture*, London, Studio Vista, 1965.

*Contemporary Sculpture, Arts Yearbook 8*, New York, The Art Digest Inc., 1965. Introduction by William Seitz.

GROHMANN, WILL. ed. *Kunst Unserer Zeit: Malerei und Plastik*, Cologne, Verlag M. Du Mont Schauberg, 1966. English edition, *New Art Around the World: Painting and Sculpture*, New York, Harry N. Abrams, Inc., 1966.

*Sculptures of the Rijksmuseum Kröller-Müller*, Otterlo, The Rijksmuseum Kröller-Müller, revised English edition, 1966; first English edition, 1963; original Dutch edition, 1952.

*Die Plastiken, Kataloge der Sonderausstellungen des Museums des 20. Jahrhunderts*, Vienna, Museum des 20. Jahrhunderts, 1966. Introduction by Dr. Werner Hofmann.

LICHT, FRED. *Sculpture 19th and 20th Centuries*, Greenwich, Connecticut, New York Graphic Society, 1967. Consultant editor John Pope-Hennessy.

## B.

### RECURRING INTERNATIONAL EXHIBITIONS
(Arranged in alphabetical order according to city)

ALTE GALERIE, MUSEUM FRIDERICHIANUM ORANGERIE, Kassel, Germany, June 27-October 5, 1964, *Documenta III, Internationale Ausstellung*.

MUSÉE CANTONAL DES BEAUX ARTS, Lausanne.
June-September, 1963. *1er Salon International de Galeries-Pilotes*.
June-October, 1966, *2e Salon Internationale de Galeries-Pilotes*.

LONDON COUNTY COUNCIL, Battersea Park, London, *Sculpture in the Open Air*.
May-September, 1960.
May-September, 1963.
June-September, 1966.

KUNSTHISTORISCHE MUSEA OPENLUCHT VOOR BEELDHOUWKUNST, Middelheim, Belgium.
July 15-October 15, 1961, *6e Biennale voor Beeldhouwkunst*.
June 8-September 30, 1963, *7e Biennale voor Beeldhouwkunst*.
June 20-September 30, 1965, *8e Biennale voor Beeldhouwkunst*.
June 11-October 2, 1967, *9e Biennale voor Beeldhouwkunst*.

MUSÉE D'ART MODERNE DE LA VILLE DE PARIS, Paris.
September-October, 1961, *IIème Biennale de Paris*.
September-October, 1963, *IIIème Biennale de Paris*.
September 28-November 3, 1965, *IVème Biennale de Paris*.

MUSÉE D'ART MODERNE DE LA VILLE DE PARIS, Paris.
May 8-29, 1960, *XVI Salon de Mai*. Also exhibited at KUNSTHAUS ZURICH, Zurich, June 11-July 24, 1960.
May 7-28, 1961, *XVII Salon de Mai*. Also exhibited at STEDELIJK MUSEUM, Amsterdam, June 7-July 7, 1961.
May, 1962 *XVIII Salon de Mai*.
April 28-May 19, 1963, *XIX Salon de Mai*.
May, 1964, *XX Salon de Mai*.
May, 1965, *XXI Salon de Mai*.
May 2-22, 1966, *XXII Salon de Mai*.
April 29-May 21, 1967, *XXIII Salon de Mai*.

MUSÉE D'ART MODERNE DE LA VILLE DE PARIS, Paris.
April 4-May 1, 1960, *15ème Salon des Réalités Nouvelles*.
June, 1961, *16ème Salon des Réalités Nouvelles*.
April 7-29, 1962, *17ème Salon des Réalités Nouvelles*.
February 2-24, 1963, *18ème Salon des Réalités Nouvelles*.
February, 1964, *19éme Salon des Réalités Nouvelles*.
March, 1965, *20ème Salon des Réalités Nouvelles*.
October 7-30, 1966, *21ème Salon des Réalités Nouvelles*.
April, 1967, *22ème Salon des Réalités Nouvelles*.

MUSÉE RODIN, Paris.
June-September, 1961, *2ème Exposition Internationale de Sculpture Contemporaine*.
June-September, 1966, *3ème Exposition Internationale de Sculpture Contemporaine*.

MUSÉE RODIN, Paris.
May 4-June 3, 1960, *XIIème Salon de la Jeune Sculpture*.
April-May, 1961, *XIIIème Salon de la Jeune Sculpture*.
April-May, 1962, *XIVème Salon de la Jeune Sculpture*.
April 26-May 25, 1963, *XVème Salon de la Jeune Sculpture*.
GALERIE D. CREUZE, Paris, June 12-July 8, 1964, *XVIème Salon de la Jeune Sculpture*.
MUSÉE RODIN, Paris, April 29-May 30, 1965, *XVIIème Salon de la Jeune Sculpture*.
FESTIVAL DU MARAIS, Paris, June-September, 1966, *XVIIIème Salon de la Jeune Sculpture*.
PALAIS ROYAL, Paris, June-September, 1967, *XIXème Salon de la Jeune Sculpture*.

DEPARTMENT OF FINE ARTS, CARNEGIE INSTITUTE, Pittsburgh, October 27, 1961-January 7, 1962, *The 1961 Pittsburgh International Exhibition of Contemporary Painting and Sculpture*.
MUSEUM OF ART, CARNEGIE INSTITUTE, Pittsburgh, October 30, 1964-January 10, 1965, *The 1964 Pittsburgh International Exhibition of Contemporary Painting and Sculpture*.

# C.

## NON-RECURRING INTERNATIONAL SCULPTURE EXHIBITIONS
(Arranged in chronological order)

PALAZZO DEL KURZAL, Republic of San Marino, July 7-September 20, 1963, *IV Biennale Internationale d'Arte*.

VI BIENAL DE SÃO PAULO, São Paulo, Brazil, September-December, 1961.

VII BIENAL DE SÃO PAULO, São Paulo, Brazil, September-December, 1963.

VIII BIENAL DE SÃO PAULO, São Paulo, Brazil, September-December, 1965.

IX BIENAL DE SÃO PAULO, São Paulo, Brazil, September-December, 1967.

THE TOKYO METROPLITAN ART GALLERY, Tokyo.
May 10-30, 1961, *The VI Tokyo Biennale*.
May 10-30, 1963, *The VII Tokyo Biennale*.
May 10-31, 1965, *The VIII Tokyo Biennale*.
May 10-31, 1967, *The IX Tokyo Biennale*.

XXX BIENNALE INTERNAZIONALE D'ARTE, Venice, June 18-October 16, 1960.

XXXI BIENNALE INTERNAZIONALE D'ARTE VENEZIA, Venice, June 16-October 7, 1962.

XXXII BIENNALE INTERNAZIONALE D'ARTE VENEZIA, Venice, June 20-October 18, 1964.

XXXIII BIENNALE INTERNAZIONALE D'ARTE VENEZIA, Venice, June 18-October 16, 1966.

GALERIJA SUVREMENE UMJETNOSTI, Zagreb, Yugoslavia.
1961, *Nove Tendencije*.
August 1-September 15, 1963, *Nove Tendencije 2*.
August 13-September 19, 1965, *Nova Tendencija 3*.

UNIVERSITY OF CALIFORNIA, Berkeley, March 6-April 3, 1960, *Art from Ingres to Pollock: Painting and Sculpture since Neo-Classicism*. Texts by Grace McCann Morley, James D. Hart, Stephen C. Pepper, Herschel B. Chipp.

MUSEUM BOYMANS-VAN BEUNINGEN, Rotterdam, March 25-September 25, 1960, *Beeldententoonstelling Floriade*.

MUSÉE CANTINI, Marseille, April, 1960, *Sculpture Contemporaine*.

MUSÉE D'ART ET D'INDUSTRIE, Saint-Etienne, Summer 1960, *Cent Sculpteurs de Daumier à nos jours*. Text by Maurice Allemand.

PARC DES EXPOSITIONS, Paris, October, 1960, *Festival d'Art Avant-Garde*.

THE CLEVELAND MUSEUM OF ART, Cleveland, Ohio, October 5-November 13, 1960, *Paths of Abstract Art*. Texts by Edward B. Henning.

STEDELIJK MUSEUM, Amsterdam, December 16, 1960-January 16, 1961, *Van Natuur tot Kunst*. Statements by individual artists.

OTTO GERSON GALLERY, New York, May-June, 1961, *The Nude in Sculpture*.

STEDELIJK MUSEUM, Amsterdam, July 22-September 11, 1961, *Polariteit:het Appolinische en het Dionysische in de Kunst*. Texts by Thomas Grochowiak and Anneliese Schröder.

THE NEW SCHOOL ART CENTER, New School for Social Research, New York, October 5-27, 1961, *Mechanism and Organism*.

GALERIE DENISE RENÉ, Paris, December, 1961-February, 1962, *Art Abstrait Constructif International*. Text Michael Seuphor.

KRESGE ART CENTER, Michigan State University, East Lansing, Michigan, December 23, 1961-January 22, 1962, *Contemporary Trends in Painting and Sculpture*.

STAEMPFLI GALLERY, New York, January 2-20, 1962, *Twenty Sculptors*.

WORLD HOUSE GALLERIES, New York, February 20-March 17, 1962, *Sculpture: Daumier to Picasso*.

MUSÉE DES ARTS DÉCORATIFS, Paris, Opened March 7, 1962, *Antagonismes 2; L'Objet*. Texts by Georges Braque and Francis Ponge.

SEATTLE WORLD'S FAIR, Seattle, April 21-October 21, 1962, *Art Since 1950*.

MUSÉE MUNICIPAL, Le Havre, May-June, 1962, *Sculpture Contemporaine*.

PROVIDENCE ART CLUB, Providence, Rhode Island, May 13-June 8, 1962, *Some Directions in Modern Sculpture*.

OTTO GERSON GALLERY, New York, June-July, 1962, *Monumental Sculpture*. Text by Michel Seuphor (excerpts from Seuphor, *Sculpture of this Century*, New York, George Braziller, 1960).

BIENNALE INTERNAZIONALE DI SCULTURA, July 15-September 2, 1962, *3 premio Carrara*.

PALAZZO COLLICOLA, Spoleto, Italy, June-September, 1962, *Festival of Two Worlds: Sculpture in the City*.

CENTRO DE ARTES VISUALES DEL INSTITUTO TORCUATO DI TELLA, Buenos Aires, September, 1962, *Premio Internacional de Escultura*.

MARTHA JACKSON GALLERY, New York, November 23-December 29, 1962, *Sculpture: International*.

PAUL ROSENBERG AND CO., New York, January 8-February 13, 1963, *American and European Sculpture*.

GALERIE CREUZE, Paris, January 19-February 19, 1963, *Actualité de la Sculpture*. Texts by Denys Chevalier, Simone Frigerio, Gérald Gassiot-Talabot, Pierre Guéguen.

GALERIE DENISE RENÉ, Paris, May-September, 1963, *Esquisse d'un Salon*. Texts by Jacques Lassaigne and Jean-Clarence Lambert.

AMERICAN ARTISTS AND STUDENTS CENTER, Paris, June 6-July 31, 1963, *Sculpture Champêtre*.

MUSEUM DES 20. JAHRHUNDERTS, Vienna, July 5-September 1, 1963, *Idole und Dämonen*. Texts by W. Hofmann and Gerhart Rindauer.

THE WASHINGTON GALLERY OF MODERN ART, Washington, D.C., September 17-October 31, 1963, *Sculptors of our Time*. Texts by Adelyn Breeskin and Andrew S. Keck.

MUSEUM DES 20. JAHRHUNDERTS, Vienna, September 21-November 4, 1962, *Kunst von 1900 bis Heute*. Text by Werner Hofmann.

MODERNA MUSEET, Stockholm, October-November, 1963, *Skulptur, Bo Boustedts Samling.* Circulated to LUNDS KONSTHALL, Lunds, Sweden; Humlebaek, Denmark, 1964; STEDELIJK MUSEUM, Amsterdam, May 1-June 1, 1964.

THE SOLOMON R. GUGGENHEIM MUSEUM, New York, October 3, 1962-January 6, 1963, *Modern Sculpture from the Joseph H. Hirshhorn Collection.* Text by H. H. Arnason.

ALBRIGHT-KNOX ART GALLERY, Buffalo, November 19-December 15, 1963, *Mixed Media and Pop Art.* Text by Gordon M. Smith.

THE MUSEUM OF FINE ARTS, Houston, Texas, January 24-February 14, 1963, *Space and Fantasy.* Statement by James Johnson Sweeney.

OTTO GERSON GALLERY, New York, May 18-June 15, 1963, *10 Sculptors in 10 Media.*

BUNDY ART GALLERY, Waitsfield, Vermont, June-August, 1963, *Sculpture Exhibition 1963.*

GÖTEBORGS KONSTMUSEUM, Göteborg, Sweden, June 10-September 1, 1963, *Konst efter 1945.*

WADSWORTH ATHENEUM, Hartford, January 9-February 9, 1964, *Black, White and Gray.* Text by Samuel J. Wagstaff, Jr.

SIDNEY JANIS GALLERY, New York, February 4-29, 1964, *The Classic Spirit in 20th Century Art.*

STAEMPFLI GALLERY, New York, February 25-March 21, 1964, *Stone, Wood, Metal.*

TATE GALLERY, London, April 22-June 28, 1964, *Painting and Sculpture of a Decade: 54-64.*

MUSEUM DES 20. JAHRHUNDERTS, Vienna, July 3-August 30, 1964, *Meisterwerke der Plastik.* Text by Werner Hofmann.

MUSEUM DES 20. JAHRHUNDERTS, Vienna, September 19-October 31, 1964, *Pop etc.* Texts by Werner Hofmann and Otto A. Graf.

THE NEW SCHOOL ART CENTER, New School for Social Research, New York, October 14-November 14, 1964, *The Artist's Reality: An International Sculpture Exhibition.* Text by Paul Mocsanyi. Statements by the artists.

*International Art Exhibition,* Lusaka, Zambia, October 19-November 30, 1964.

AKADEMIE DER KÜNSTE, Berlin, November 24, 1964-January 3, 1965, *Neue Realisten und Pop Art.* Text by Werner Hofmann.

STAEMPFLI GALLERY, New York, February 23-March 20, 1965, *Stone and Crystal.*

ALBRIGHT-KNOX ART GALLERY, Buffalo, February 27-March 28, 1965, *Kinetic and Optic Art Today.* Text by Gordon M. Smith.

LUNDS KONSTHALL, Lunds, Sweden, March 19-April 25, 1965, *Le Merveilleux Moderne.*

PROVIDENCE ART CLUB, Providence, Rhode Island, March 31-April 24, 1965, *1965 Kane Memorial Art Exhibition, Critics Choice: Art Since World War II.* Texts by Thomas B. Hess, H. Kramer, H. Rosenberg.

VONDELPARK, Amsterdam, April 1-October 1, 1965, *Sculptuur in Amsterdam.* Text by W. Sandberg, (French, German, English translations).

STEDELIJK MUSEUM, Amsterdam, April 15-June 8, 1965, *Nul Negentienhonderd Vijf en Zestig.* Two volumes. Excerpts from statements and writings of the artists.

DALLAS MUSEUM OF FINE ARTS, Dallas, Texas, May 12-June 13, 1965, *Sculpture Twentieth Century.*

JARDIN BOTANIQUE, Montreal, July-August, 1965, *Confrontation 65; International Exhibition of Sculpture.* Texts by Yves Robillard and Robert Ayre.

HILL OF THE MUSES, Athens, September 8-November 8, 1965, *1st International Biennale of World Sculpture, Panathenea of World Sculpture.*

HAAGS GEMEENTEMUSEUM, The Hague, October 20-November 21, 1965, *Verzameling Bär, Zurich, Beeldhouwwerken en Tekeningen.*

WORLD HOUSE GALLERY, New York, November 3-27, 1965, *Sculpture from all Directions.*

MUSÉE D'ART MODERNE DE LA VILLE DE PARIS, Paris, December, 1965, *Un Groupe 1965.* Texts by René Héron de Villefosse and André Chastel.

GALERIE CLAUDE BERNARD, Paris, December 14, 1965, *La Main: sculptures.*

UNIVERSITY ART MUSEUM, The University of New Mexico, Albuquerque, March 25-May 1, 1966, *Twentieth Century Sculpture.*

CORDIER AND EKSTROM, INC., New York, April 26-May 21, 1966, *Seven Decades, 1865-1965: Crosscurrents in Modern Art: 1955-1965,* Organized by the Public Education Association. Text by Peter Selz.

WESTFALISCHER KUNSTVEREIN, Münster, Germany, May 8-June 19, 1966, *Tendenzen Strukturaler Kunst.* Text by Jurgen Wissmann.

5e INTERNATIONALE BEELDENTENTOONSTELLUNG, Sonsbeek, The Netherlands, May 27-September 25, 1966.

STÄDISCHES MUSEUM, Leverkusen, Germany, June 13-July 19, 1966, *Tradition und Gegenwart.* Texts by Rolf Wedwer, Fredrich Hommel, Hans Neinz Holz, Hans Meyer, Georges Schlocker.

HANOVER GALLERY LTD., London, June 28-September 9, 1966, *The Poetic Image.*

DE CORDOVA MUSEUM, Lincoln, Massachusetts, June 29-September 4, 1966, *Outdoor Sculpture '66.*

MUSEO NACIONAL DE BELLA ARTES, Buenos Aires, September, 1966, *Plástica con Plásticos.*

MASSACHUSETTS INSTITUTE OF TECHNOLOGY, Boston, September 14-October 10, 1966, *Sculpture from the Collection of Mr. and Mrs. Max Wasserman.* Text by William C. Seitz.

CENTRO DE ARTES VISUALES DEL INSTITUTO TORCUATO DI TELLA, Buenos Aires, September 29-October 30, 1966, *Premio Nacional Instituto Torcuato di Tella.* Texts by L.A. (Lawrence Alloway), Otto Hahn, Jorge Romero Brest, David Lamelas, Susana Salgado.

STEDELIJK MUSEUM, Amsterdam, November 19, 1966—January 15, 1967, *Vormen van de Kleur.* Texts by E. de Wilde and W. A. L. Beeren.

EXPO 67, Montreal, Canada, April-October, 1967, *International Exhibition of Contemporary Sculpture.*

ART INSTITUTE OF CHICAGO, Chicago, June 23-August 23, 1967, *Sculpture: A Generation of Innovation.*

# II. BIBLIOGRAPHY AND EXHIBITIONS BY COUNTRY

## AUSTRIA

### Books and articles

VON DER OSTEN, G. *Plastik des 20. Jahrhunderts in Deutschland, Österreich und der Schweiz*, Königstein im Taunus, Verlag Karl Robert Langewiesche, Die Blauen Bücher, 1963.

BREICHA, OTTO. "Neue Wege der Österreichischen Plastik", *Kunstwerk*, Baden-Baden, vol. 18, no. 6, December, 1964, pp. 11-18.

BREICHA, OTTO. "The New Austrian Sculpture: An Attempt at a Survey", *Studio International*, London, vol. 170, no. 872, December, 1965, pp. 220-227.

SOTRIFFER, KRISTIAN. *Modern Austrian Art*, New York, Frederick A. Praeger, 1965. Translated from the German by Alisa Jaffa. German edition, Vienna, Anton Schroll and Co., 1963.

HOFMANN, WERNER. *Moderne Kunst in Österreich*, Vienna, 1965.

MUSCHIK, JOHANN. *Österreichische Plastik*, Vienna, 1966.

### Exhibitions

ARTS COUNCIL OF GREAT BRITAIN, London, May 4-June 4, 1960, *Austrian Painting and Sculpture 1900 to 1960*. Introduction by Werner Hofmann.

KÜNSTLERHAUS, Graz, Austria, September-October, 1963, *Trigon '63*.

KÜNSTLERHAUS, Graz, Austria, September-October, 1965, *Trigon '65*.

## BELGIUM

### Exhibitions

GALERIE MÜLLER, Stuttgart, October 21-November 21, 1963, *Aktuelle Belgische Kunst*.

STÄDTISCHE KÜNSTGALERIE, Bochum, Germany, April 21-May 19, 1963, *Profil II: Belgische Kunst Heute*.

WÜRTTEMBERGISCHER KUNSTVEREIN, Stuttgart, October 19-November 24, 1963, *Belgische Kunst vor der Jahrhundertwende bis Gegenwart*.

FINCH COLLEGE MUSEUM OF ART, New York, January 9-February 27, 1965, *Art from Belgium*. Also exhibited at THE STAMFORD MUSEUM, Stamford, Connecticut, February 6-27, 1965.

## CANADA

### Books and articles

"Sculpture in Canada", *Canadian Art*, Toronto, vol. XIX, no. 4, July-August, 1962, pp. 268-295. Includes "An Editorial" by Alan Jarvis; "Painter-Sculptors" by Elizabeth Kilbourn; "Welders" by Evan H. Turner; "Carvers" by David P. Silcox; "Modellers" by Lawrence Sabbath.

GREENBERG, CLEMENT. "Clement Greenberg's View of Art on the Prairies", *Canadian Art*, Toronto, issue no. 84, vol. XX, no. 2, March, 1963, pp. 90-108. ("Sculpture" section pp. 105-107.)

MCPHERSON, HUGO. "Scope of Sculpture in '64", *Canadian Art*, Toronto, issue no. 92, vol. XXI, no. 4, July, 1964, pp. 224-235.

LORD, BARRY. "Canadian Sculptors at Expo", *Artscanada*, issue no. 108, vol. XXIV, no. 5, May, 1967. pp. 12-16.

MCPHERSON, HUGO. *Painting and Sculpture, The Canadians*, Galt, Ontario, The Macmillan Company of Canada Ltd., 1967.

### Exhibitions

NATIONAL GALLERY OF CANADA, Ottawa, Summer 1962, *Canadian Outdoor Sculpture Exhibition 1962*. Statements by Charles F. Comfort, and by jury members Lynn Chadwick, Elizabeth Wynn Wood, and Armand Vaillancourt.

THE INTERNATIONAL COUNCIL OF THE MUSEUM OF MODERN ART, New York, 1963-1964, *Fifteen Canadian Artists*. Texts by Evan H. Turner and William J. Withrow.

DOROTHY CAMERON GALLERY, Toronto, (Part I), March 20-April 5, (Part II), April 10-April 26, 1964, *Canadian Sculpture Today*.

NATIONAL GALLERY OF CANADA, Ottawa, Summer 1964, *Deuxième Exposition de Sculpture Canadienne*.

DOROTHY CAMERON GALLERY, Toronto, January 29-February 15, 1965, *New Directions in Canadian Sculpture*.

RODMAN HALL ARTS CENTRE, St. Catherine, Ontario, Canada, February 6-March 2, 1966. *Canadian Sculpture / 1916-1966*.

CITY HALL OF TORONTO, Toronto, June 1-September 5, 1967, *An Open Air Exhibition of Canadian Sculpture*.

## CZECHOSLOVAKIA

### Books and articles

FRY, EDWARD F. "A Central European Miscellany", *Artforum*, San Francisco, vol. IV, no. 8, April, 1966, pp. 23-26.

*Výtvarné umĕni* (Fine Arts), Prague, no. 6-7, 1966. Special issue devoted to contemporary Czechoslovakian art.

### Exhibitions

ZAHRADA OBLASTNÍ GALERIE, BOTANICKÁ ZAHRADA, Liberec, Czechoslovakia, July-September, 1964, *Socha 1964*. (The Gardens of the Regional Gallery, Botanical Garden, *Sculpture 1964*.)

OBLASTNÍ GALERIE, Olomouc, Czechoslovakia, August-September, 1965, *Socharská Bilance: 1955-1965*. (Regional Gallery, *Sculptural Summary: 1955-1965*.)

STÄDTISCHE KUNSTGALERIE, Bochum, Germany, May 16-July 25, 1965, *Tschechoslowakische Kunst heute / Profil V*. Text by Jiří Kotalík and Miroslav Mĩčko.

AKADEMIE DER KÜNSTE, Berlin, July 17-August 21, 1966, *Tschechoslowakische Kunst der Gegenwart*. Text by Hans Scharoun and Jindrich Chalupecký.

MUSEUM FOLKWANG, Essen, Germany, October 16-November 27, 1966, *Tschechoslowakische Plastik von 1900 bis zur Gegenwart*. Texts by Paul Vogt and Petr Hartmann-Vázlav Procázka.

OBLASTNÍ GALERIE, Liberec, Czechoslovakia, 1966, *Slovenská Socha 1966*. (Regional Gallery, Liberec, *Slovak Sculpture*, 1966).

## FRANCE

### Books and articles

GINDERTAL, R. V., "Situations actuelles de la sculpture dans le cadre de l'École de Paris", *Quadrum*, Brussels, no. 12, 1961, pp. 21-44, 189.

MARCHIORI, GIUSEPPE, *Modern French Sculpture*, New York, Harry N. Abrams, Inc., 1963, Translated from the Italian by John Ross. Italian edition, *Scultura Francese Moderna*, Milan, Silvana Editoriale d'Arte, 1963.

ASHBERY, JOHN. "Paris Sculptors", *Art News Annual*, New York, no. XXX, 1965, pp. 144-157, 175-180.

### Exhibitions

See above, under "Recurring International Exhibitions" and "Non-Recurring International Sculpture Exhibitions", exhibitions held in Paris, Marseille, St. Etienne, and Le Havre.

## GERMANY

### Books and articles

ROH, FRANZ. "Zur neuen plastik in Deutschland", *Werk*, Winterthur, vol. 47, no. 3, March, 1960, pp. 104-108.

KULTERMANN, UDO. *Junge Deutsche Bildhauer*, Mainz, Florian Kupferberg Verlag, 1963.

VON DER OSTEN, G. *Plastik des 20. Jahrhunderts in Deutschland, Österreich und der Schweiz*, Königstein im Taunus, Verlag Karl Robert Langewiesche, Die Blauen Bücher, 1963.

DE LA MOTTE, MANFRED. "Plastik in Deutschland", *Art International*, Lugano, vol. X, no. 7, September 15, 1966, pp. 25-28+.

### Exhibitions

HAUS DER KUNST, Munich, June 25-October 9, 1960, *Grosse Kunstausstellung / München, 1960*.

HAUS DER KUNST, Munich, June 6-October 1, 1961, *Grosse Kunstausstellung / München 1961*.

STAATLICHE KUNSTHALLE, Baden-Baden, April 2-14, 1961, *Deutscher Künstlerbund / Elfte Ausstellung*.

STÄDTISCHES MUSEUM, Leverkusen, Germany, May 5-June 6, 1961, *30 Junge Deutsche*. Introduction by Udo Kultermann.

HAUS DER KUNST, Munich, June 9-October 7, 1962, *Grosse Kunstausstellung / München 1962*.

MUSEO DE ARTE CONTEMPORANEO, Universidad de Chile, Santiago, August 1962, *Arte Actual Alemán*. Introduction by Karl Hartung.

HAUS DER KUNST, Munich, June 12-October 6, 1963, *Grosse Kunstausstellung / München 1963*.

WÜRTTEMBERGISCHER KUNSTVEREIN, Stuttgart, May 18-June 30, 1963, *Deutscher Künstlerbund/Zwölfte Ausstellung*. Statement by Karl Hartung.

HAUS DER KUNST, Munich, June 5-September 27, 1964, *Grosse Kunstausstellung / München, 1964*.

HAUS AM WALDSEE, Berlin, March 21-May 3, 1964, *Möglichkeiten* (a section of *Deutscher Künstlerbund, 13. Ausstellung*.)

HOCHSCHULE FÜR BILDENDE KÜNSTE, Berlin, March 21-May 3, 1964, *Jahresausstellung* (a section of *Deutscher Künstlerbund, 13. Ausstellung*).

KUNSTVEREIN, Augsburg, Germany, February 22-April 5, 1964, *Deutsche Bildhauer der Gegenwart*.

MUSÉE NATIONAL D'ART MODERNE, Paris, 1964, *L'Art jeune contemporain en Allemagne*. Text by Dr. Franz Roh. An exhibition arranged for the 10th *Salon Comparisons* by the Gesellschaft der Freunde junger Kunst, Munich, under the direction of Dr. Franz Roh.

HAUS DER KUNST, Munich, June 24-August 3, 1965, *Grosse Kunstausstellung/München 1965*.

KUNSTHALLE, Mannheim, December 15, 1965-January 16, 1966, *Biennale Paris 1965. Die Jungen Deutschen*. Text by Thomas Grochowiak.

AKADEMIE DER KÜNSTE, Berlin, June 5-July 10, 1966, *Junge Generation*. Introduction by Will Grohmann.

HAUS DER KUNST, Munich, June 9-September 25, 1966, *Grosse Kunstausstellung / München 1966*.

STAATLICHE KUNSTHALLE, Baden-Baden, March 4-June 10, 1966, *Plastik Südwest*. Introduction by Kurt Leonhard.


## ISRAEL

### Books and articles

DUBINER, SAMUEL and FISCHER, YONA. "L'Art Israélein D'Aujourd'hui," *Aujourd'hui*, Boulogne-sur-Seine, no. 26, April, 1960, pp. 11-27.

KUH, KATHERINE. "The Art that History Shaped", *Saturday Review*, New York, January 29, 1966, pp. 17-24.

### Exhibitions

MUSÉE NATIONAL D'ART MODERNE, Paris, May 1960, *Art Israëlien Contemporain*.

THE INTERNATIONAL COUNCIL OF THE MUSEUM OF MODERN ART, New York, 1964, *Art Israel: 26 Painters and Sculptors*. Text by William C. Seitz.

THE ISRAEL MUSEUM, Jerusalem, May 11-June 28, 1965, *Trends in Israeli Art*. Catalogue by Yona Fischer.


## ITALY

### Books and articles

SALVINI, ROBERTO. *Modern Italian Sculpture*, New York, Harry N. Abrams, Inc., 1961.

MANDEL, GABRIELE. ed., *Scultura italiana contemporanea*, Milan, Instituto Europeo di Storia d'Arte, 1965.

CHEVALIER, DENYS. "Les Sculpteurs italiens de Paris", *Aujourd'hui*, Boulogne-sur-Seine, no. 48, January, 1965, pp. 70-71.

CRISPOLTI, ENRICO. "Perspectives et personalités de la jeune sculpture en Italie", *Aujourd'hui*, Boulogne-sur-Seine, no. 48, January, 1965, pp. 62-65.

KALAJIĆ, DRAGOŠ. "Italijanska sculptura danas" ("Italian Sculpture Today") , *Umetnost*, Belgrade, no. 2, April-June, 1965, pp. 112-126.

ALFIERI, BRUNO, and MARCHIORI, GIUSEPPE. "La nuova scultura italiana: Icaro, Lorenzetti, Pierelli, Pizzo Greco, Remotti", *Metro*, Milan, no. 11, June, 1966, pp. 76-101.

BARO, GENE. "Sculpture—Italian Style", *Art and Artists*, London, vol. 1, no. 7, October. 1966, pp. 16-19.

DELL'ARCO, MAURIZIO FAGIOLO. *Rapporto 60: Le Arti Oggi in Italia*, Rome, Mario Bulzoni, Editore, 1966.

LOY, NANNI. *Nuova Scultura Italiana*, Campobasso, Italy, Nocera Editore, 1966. Recorded conversations with seven artists.

### Exhibitions

MUSÉE RODIN, Paris, June, 1960, *Sculpture Italienne Contemporaine d'Arturo Martini à nos jours*. Preface by Rodolfo Palluchini.

NEUE GALERIE DER STADT LINZ, Linz, Austria, August 5-31, 1960, *Italienische Kunst der Gegenwart*. Introduction by G. C. Argan.

CASA ITALIANA, COLUMBIA UNIVERSITY, New York, October-November 10, 1961, *Contemporary Italian Sculpture*. Introduction by Enzo Carli. Exhibition organized by the Casa Italiana and the Livorno Art Center, in cooperation with the American Federation of Arts and the American Italy Society.

THE DALLAS MUSEUM FOR CONTEMPORARY ARTS, Dallas, October, 1960, *Italian Sculptors of Today*. Introduction by Lionello Venturi, translated from the Italian by Dorothy Cater. "A Note on the Selection", by Douglas MacAgy.

GÖTEBORGS KONSTMUSEUM, Göteborg, Norway, June 21-July 23, 1961, *Italiensk Kultur I Dag*. Text by Alfred Westholm.

ISAAC DELGADO MUSEUM OF ART, New Orleans, January, 1961, *Contemporary Italian Sculptors*.

KUNSTNERNES HUS, Oslo, May 9-June 11, 1961, *Italiensk Kunst I Dag*. Statements by Alf-Jørgin Aas, Gian Alberto Dell'Acqua, Guido Ballo, Franco Russoli, Umbro Appolonio.

MODERNA GALERIJA, Ljubljana, Yugoslavia, November, 1961, *Premio Morgan's Paint: III mednarodni biennale Slikarstva in kiparstva*. Texts by Francesco Archangeli, Zoran Kržišnik, Eugenio Riccomini.

TAKASHIMAYA DEPARTMENT STORE, Tokyo, January 17-29, 1961, *Italian Contemporary Sculpture*.

KÜNSTLERHAUS, Graz, Austria, September-October, 1963, *Trigon '63*.

KÜNSTLERHAUS, Graz, Austria, September-October, 1965, *Trigon '65*.

*Contemporary Italian Sculpture*, Aukland, Wellington, Christchurch, and Dundex, New Zealand, September, 1965-January, 1966. Text by Fortunato Bellonzi.

MUSEUM BOYMANS VAN BEUNINGEN, Rotterdam, November 26, 1965-January 16, 1966, *Twaalf Italiaanse beeldhouwers*. Text by Eduard Trier.

DOM GALERIE, Cologne, December, 1966, *Plastik und Schmuck: Italienscher Künstler*.

ARTS GUILD OF GREAT BRITAIN, Edinburgh, Scotland, August 13-September 18, 1966, *Twenty Italian Sculptors*.

GALLERIA ARCO D'ALIBERT, Rome, May 30- June 26, 1966, *La nuova scultura Italiana*.

GALLERIA LA POLENA, Genoa, October 29-November 30, 1966, *Nuova Scultura Italiana*.

GALLERIA NAZIONALE D'ARTE MODERNA, Rome, March-April, 1966. *Aspetti dell'arte Italiana Contemporanea*.

MUSEO DE ARTE MODERNO, Mexico City, 1966, *Arte Italiano Contemporaneo Desde 1910*. Exhibition organized for the "Quadriennale" of Rome. Text by Fortunato Bellonzi.

SOUTHERN METHODIST UNIVERSITY, Dallas, April, 1966, *Modern Italian Sculpture*. Text by Roberto Salvini.

## JAPAN

### Books and articles

HAMAMURA, JUN. "New Trends in Sculpture", *Mizue*, Tokyo, January, 1964, pp. 81-84. (English summary).

KUNG, DAVID. *The Contemporary Artist in Japan*, Honolulu, East-West Center Press, 1966. Japanese edition, Bijutsu Shuppansha, Tokyo.

### Exhibitions

*The Fourth Annual Contemporary Art Exhibition of Japan*, Tokyo, May, 1960. Under the Auspices of the Mainichi Shimbun.

*The Fifth Annual Contemporary Art Exhibition of Japan*, Tokyo, May, 1962. Under the Auspices of the Mainichi Shimbun.

"Escultura japonêsa, Escultura japonêsa de pos-guerra; materiais usados na escultura japonêsa", *Habitat*, São Paulo, vol. 12, no. 69, September, 1962, pp. 56-59.

THE NATIONAL MUSEUM OF MODERN ART, Tokyo, May 17-June 16, 1963, *New Generation of Japanese Sculptors*. Text in English.

TOKIWA PARK, UBE CITY, Japan, September 10-November 11, 1963, *First Exhibition of All Japan Sculpture*.

THE NATIONAL MUSEUM OF MODERN ART, Kyoto, April 4-May 10, 1964, *Contemporary Trend of Japanese Paintings and Sculptures*. Text in English.

THE MUSEUM OF MODERN ART, Kamakura, Japan, October 9-14, 1964, *Exhibition of Japanese Sculpture*.

THE NATIONAL MUSEUM OF MODERN ART, Tokyo, October 1-November 8, 1964, *Masterpieces of Modern Japanese Art*. Text by Michiaki Kawakita (translations in English and French).

*The Sixth Annual Contemporary Art Exhibition of Japan*, Tokyo, May, 1964. Under the Auspices of Mainichi Shimbun.

THE MUSEUM OF MODERN ART, New York, October 17-December 26, 1966, *The New Japanese Painting and Sculpture*. Text by William S. Lieberman. Also exhibited at SAN FRANCISCO MUSEUM OF ART, April 29-June 13, 1965; DENVER ART MUSEUM, October 2-November 14, 1965; KRANNERT ART MUSEUM, University of Illinois, Urbana, Illinois, December 12, 1965-January 30, 1966; JOSLYN ART MUSEUM, Omaha, February 26-March 20, 1966; THE COLUMBUS GALLERY OF FINE ARTS, Columbus, Ohio, April 7-May 6, 1966; THE BALTIMORE MUSEUM OF ART, January 24-March 19, 1967; MILWAUKEE ART CENTER, April 13-May 14, 1967.

THE NATIONAL MUSEUM OF MODERN ART, Kyoto, June 18-July 25, 1965, *Contemporary Trend of Japanese Paintings and Sculpture*.

GUTAI PINACOTHECA, Osaka, Japan, October, 1965, *Gutai 14, 15th Gutai Art Exhibition*. Text by Jiro Yoshihara.

TOKIWA PARK, Ube City, Japan, October 1-31, 1965. *The First Exhibition of Modern Japanese Sculptures*.

THE NATIONAL MUSEUM OF MODERN ART, Tokyo, January 21-February 27, 1966, *New Generation of Contemporary Art*. Statement by Tamon Miki (translation in English).

JAPAN ART FESTIVAL ASSOCIATION, INC., Union Carbide Building, New York, March 22-April 23, 1966, *The First Japan Art Festival*.

*The Seventh Contemporary Art Exhibition of Japan*, Tokyo, May, 1966. Under the Auspices of the Mainichi Shimbun.

THE NATIONAL MUSEUM OF MODERN ART, Kyoto, May 10-June 5, 1966, *Trends in Contemporary Japanese Painting and Sculpture*. Text in English.

GALLERIA DEL CAVALLINO, Venice, June 15-July 15, 1966, *Modern Art of Japan*. Text by Ichiro Haryu.

THE NATIONAL MUSEUM OF MODERN ART, Kyoto, October, 1966, *Dimension '66*.

## THE NETHERLANDS

### Exhibitions

STEDELIJK MUSEUM, Amsterdam, December 24, 1959-February 1, 1960, *Beelden in het Heden*. Statement by Dr. H. L. C. Jaffé.

FRITZ-HENTZLER HAUS, Dortmund, Germany, 1960, *Hollandische Plastik der Gegenwart*.

STEDELIJK MUSEUM, Amsterdam, June 29-September 17, 1962, *Nederlands Bijdrage: Tot de Internationale Ontwikkeling sedert 1945*. Also exhibited at MONTREAL MUSEUM OF FINE ARTS, October 5-November 4, 1962; THE NATIONAL GALLERY OF CANADA, Ottawa, November 15-December 31, 1962.

STEDELIJK MUSEUM, Amsterdam, July 6-September, 1963, *Nationale Herdenking 1813-1963/150 jaar Nederlandse Kunst*. Texts by Victorine Bakker-Hefting, H. L. C. Jaffé, L. Gána (on sculpture), and others. English translation by Elizabeth Williams-Treeman.

THE JEWISH MUSEUM, New York, April 1-May 1, 1963, *Holland: The New Generation*.

## POLAND

### Books and articles

LANGSNER, JULES, "Modern Art in Poland: The Legacy and the Revival", *Art International*, Zurich, vol. 5, no. 7, September 20, 1961, pp. 22-29.

### Exhibitions

I BIENNALE FORM PRZESTRZENNYCH, (I Biennial of Spatial Forms), Elblag, Poland, July 22-August 11, 1965.

## SPAIN

### Books and articles

CERNI, VICENTE AGUILERA. "La nuova scultura espagnola", *La Biennale di Venezia*, Venice, no. 40, July-September, 1960, pp. 24-31.

ZOBEL, FERNANDO. *Casas Colgadas. Museo Cuenca: Colleccion de Arte Abstracto Español*, Madrid, 1966. Catalogue of the permanent collection of the Museo de las Casas Colgadas de Cuenca, Spain.

### Exhibitions

MUSEUM OF MODERN ART, New York, July 20-September 28, 1960, *New Spanish Painting and Sculpture*. Introduction by Frank O'Hara. Also exhibited at THE CORCORAN GALLERY OF ART, Washington, D.C., October 31-November 28, 1960; THE COLUMBUS GALLERY OF FINE ARTS, Columbus, Ohio, January 3-31, 1961; WASHINGTON UNIVERSITY, St. Louis, February 16-March 16, 1961; LOWE ART GALLERY, University of Miami, Coral Gables, Florida, April 1-29, 1961; MARION KOOGLER MCNAY ART INSTITUTE, San Antonio, Texas, May 15-June 12, 1961; ISAAC DELGADO MUSEUM OF ART, New Orleans, September 18-October 16, 1961; THE CONTEMPORARY ART CENTER, Cincinnati, November 1-29, 1961; CURRIER GALLERY OF ART, Manchester, New Hampshire, December 15, 1961-January 12, 1962.

PALAIS DES BEAUX-ARTS, Brussels, March, 1961, *Art Espagnol Contemporain*.

MARLBOROUGH GALLERY, London, January, 1962, *Contemporary Spanish Painting and Sculpture*. Text by Vicente Aguilera Cerni.

D'ARCY GALLERIES, New York, April 20-May 9, 1964, *Spanish Painting and Sculpture Today, Five Artists of the Pavilion of Spain, New York World's Fair 1964-1965*.

## SWITZERLAND

### Books and articles

VON DER OSTEN, G. *Plastik des 20. Jahrhunderts in Deutschland, Österreich und der Schweiz*, Königstein in Taunus, Verlag Karl Robert Langewiesche, Die Blauen Bücher, 1963.

### Exhibitions

KUNTSMUSEUM ST. GALLEN, St. Gallen, Switzerland, May-July 17, 1960, *43 Junge Schweizer: Plastik, Malerei, Zeichnung*. Texts by E. Naegeli, R. Hanhart, P. F. Althaus. Also exhibited at STÄDTISCHE MUSEUM, Leverkusen, Germany, July 28-September 18, 1960.

PARKANLAGE AM SEE, Biel, Switzerland, June 16-July 29, 1962, *3 Schweizer Plastik-Ausstellung im Freien*.

MUSÉE RODIN, Paris, June-October, 1963, *La Sculpture en Suisse: 1952-1963*. Text by Marcel Joray.

MUSÉE CANTONAL DES BEAUX-ARTS, Lausanne, April 30-October 25, 1964, *Art Suisse au XX Siècle*.

KONGRESSHAUS, Biel, Switzerland, June 11-July 25, 1966, *4 Schweizer Plastik-Ausstellung*.

# UNITED KINGDOM

## Books and articles

RUSSELL, JOHN. "London letter: sculpture renaissance", *Art in America*, New York, vol. 48, no. 2, Summer 1960, pp. 106-108.

HODIN, DR. JOSEF PAUL. "Englische Skulptur seit Moore", *Werk*, Winterthur, vol. 48, no. 1, January, 1961, pp. 25-29; reprinted in French, *XX Siècle*, Paris, May, 1961, Supplement pp. 1-4.

MULLINS, EDWIN. "The Open-Air Vision: A Survey of sculpture in London since 1945", *Apollo*, London, vol. 77, no. 6, (new series), August, 1962, pp. 455-463.

LYNTON, NORBERT. "Latest Developments in British Sculpture", *Art and Literature*, Lausanne, Switzerland, no. 2, Summer 1964, pp. 195-211.

FARR, DENNIS. *British Sculpture Since 1945*, London, Tate Gallery, 1965.

SPENCER, CHARLES S. "The Phenomenon of British Sculpture", *Studio International*, London, vol. 169, no. 863, March, 1965, pp. 98-105.

FORGE, ANDREW. "Some New British Sculptors", *Artforum*, San Francisco, vol. 3, no. 8, May, 1965, pp. 31-35.

BARO, GENE. "Britain's New Sculpture", *Art International*, Lugano, Switzerland, vol. 9, no. 5, June, 1965, pp. 26-31.

HODIN, J. P. "The Avant-garde of English Sculpture and the Liberation from the Liberators", *Quadrum*, Brussels, no. 18, 1965, pp. 55-70.

REICHARDT, JASIA. "Colour in Sculpture", *Quadrum*, Brussels, no. 18, 1965, pp. 71-78.

BARO, GENE. "Britain's Young Sculptors", *Arts*, New York, vol. 40, no. 2, December, 1965, pp. 13-17.

DIENST, ROLF-GUNTER. "Drei Aspekte der Neuen Englischen Plastik", *Kunstwerk*, Baden-Baden, Germany, vol. 19, no. 9, March 1966, pp. 11-20.

BARO, GENE. "British sculpture: the developing scene", *Studio International*, London, vol. 172, no. 882, October, 1966, pp. 171-181.

HAMMACHER, A. M. *Modern English Sculpture*, London, Thames and Hudson, 1967.

JOUFFROY, ALAIN. "Art de Demi Brume à Londres", *L'Oeil*, Paris, no. 149, May, 1967, pp. 34-41, 84.

## Exhibitions

*Contemporary British Sculpture 1960.* An open-air exhibition organized by The Arts Council of Great Britain. Foreword by G. W.; Introduction by Ronald Pickvance. Exhibited at CANNON HILL PARK, Birmingham, April 30-May 14, 1960; ASHBURNE HALL, Manchester, June 18-July 9, 1960; AVONBANK GARDENS, Stratford-on-Avon, July 16-August 6, 1960; INVERLEITH HOUSE, Edinburgh, Scotland, August 18-September 11, 1960; Cheltenham, September 24-October 8, 1960.

*Sculpture 1961.* An exhibition organized by The Arts Council of Great Britain Welsh Committee. Introduction by Bryan Robertson. Exhibited at THE NATIONAL MUSEUM OF WALES, Cardiff, July 15-September 2, 1961; THE GLYNN VIVIAN ART GALLERY, Swansea, September 9-30, 1961; THE NATIONAL LIBRARY OF WALES, Aberystwyth, October 7-28, 1961; UNIVERSITY COLLEGE, Bangor, November 4-28, 1961.

MUSEUM OF FINE ARTS, Montreal, August 1-September 4, 1961, *British Contemporary Sculptors.*

INSTITUTE OF CONTEMPORARY ARTS, London, August 30-October 7, 1961, *26 Young Sculptors.*

*Recent British Sculpture.* An exhibition organized by the British Council, 1961-1963. Introduction by David Thompson. Circulated in Canada by the NATIONAL GALLERY OF ART, Ottawa; circulated in New Zealand by the AUKLAND CITY ART GALLERY; circulated in Australia by the STATE GALLERIES OF AUSTRALIA.

*Contemporary British Sculpture.* An exhibition organized by The Arts Council of Great Britain, 1962. Foreword by G. W.; Introduction by Ronald Pickvance. Exhibited at CAERPHILLY CASTLE, Wales, April 28-May 12, 1962; STEVENAGE COLLEGE OF FURTHER EDUCATION, May 19-June 9, 1962; ST. JOHN'S CHURCH, Chester, July 14-August 4. 1962; INVERLEITH CASTLE, Edinburgh, Scotland, August 11-September 8, 1962.

SAN FRANCISCO MUSEUM OF ART, November 13-December 16, 1962, *British Art Today.* Introduction by Lawrence Alloway. Also exhibited at DALLAS MUSEUM FOR CONTEMPORARY ARTS, January 15-February 17, 1963; SANTA BARBARA MUSEUM OF ART, March 7-April 9, 1963.

*Contemporary British Sculpture 1964.* An open-air exhibition organized by The Arts Council of Great Britain. Foreword by G. W.; Introduction by Ronald Pickvance. Exhibited at CANNON HILL PARK, *Birmingham*, April 25-May 9, 1964; HAWORTH ART GALLERY, Accrington, May 16-June 6, 1964; IMPERIAL GARDENS, Cheltenham, July 7-19, 1964; ALBERT PARK, Middlesbrough, July 25-August 15, 1964; LISTER PARK, Bradford, August 22-September 12, 1964.

STÄDTISCHE KUNSTGALERIE, Bochum, Germany, April 19-June 7, 1964, *Profile III/Englische Kunst der Gegenwart.* Introduction by Sir Herbert Read and Roland Penrose.

TATE GALLERY, London, July 15-August 16, 1964, *London Group* (1914-1964 Jubilee Exhibition, Fifty Years of British Art at the Tate Gallery). Also exhibited at NATIONAL MUSEUM OF WALES, Cardiff, August 26-September 26, 1964; MUSEUM AND GALLERY OF ART, Doncaster, England, October 10-31, 1964.

ALBRIGHT-KNOX ART GALLERY, Buffalo, New York, October 27-November 29, 1964, *Contemporary British Painting and Sculpture.*

WALKER ART CENTER, Minneapolis, February 6-March 14, 1965, *London: The New Scene.* Also exhibited at THE WASHINGTON GALLERY OF MODERN ART, Washington, D.C., April 1-May 2; INSTITUTE OF CONTEMPORARY ART, Boston, June 12-July 25; SEATTLE ART MUSEUM PAVILION, September 8-October 10; THE VANCOUVER ART GALLERY, October 30-November 28; THE ART GALLERY OF TORONTO, January 8-February 6, 1966; THE NATIONAL GALLERY OF CANADA, Ottawa, February 18-March 20.

TATE GALLERY, London, February 25-April 4, 1965, *British Sculpture in the Sixties.* Foreword by Whitney Straight; Introduction by James Melville, Bryan Robertson, and Alan Bowness.

ARTS COUNCIL GALLERY, London, February 26-March 27, 1965, *Towards Art II* (Sculptors from the Royal College of Art). Also exhibited at TORRE ABBEY, Torquay, April 10-May 1; SOUTHAMPTON ART GALLERY, May 8-29; LEEDS CITY ART GALLERY, June 5-26; MIDLAND GROUP GALLERY, Nottingham, July 3-24; BOLTON MUSEUM AND ART GALLERY, July 31-August 21; NORWICH CASTLE MUSEUM, August 28-September 18.

WHITECHAPEL GALLERY, London, March-April, 1965, *The New Generation: 1965.* Preface by Bryan Robertson; Introduction by Ian Dunlop. Also exhibited at ULSTER MUSEUM, Belfast, December 15, 1965-January 22, 1966.

*Contemporary British Sculpture 1965.* An open-air exhibition organized by The Arts Council of Great Britain. Foreword by G. W.; Introduction by Ronald Pickvance. Exhibited at CANNON HILL PARK, Birmingham, April 17-May 1; BRIGHTON UNIVERSITY, May 8-29; ABINGTON PARK, Northampton, June 3-26; CASTLE GROUNDS, Nottingham, July 3-24; BOWES MUSEUM, Barnard Castle, July 31-August 30; HILLFIELD GARDENS, Gloucester, September 4-25.

MARLBOROUGH-GERSON GALLERY, New York, November 22-December 31, 1965, *The English Eye.* Texts by Robert Melville and Bryan Robertson.

NATIONAL MUSEUM OF WALES, Cardiff, June 16-July 30, 1966, *Structure 1966.* Introduction by Peter Jones. Also exhibited at GLYNN VIVIAN ART GALLERY, Swansea, August 6-27; ART GALLERY, Bangor, September 3-24; ARTS COUNCIL GALLERY, London, October 1-22; PENWITH GALLERY, St. Ives, November 12-December 3; ART GALLERY, Leicester, December 10-30; WHITWORTH ART GALLERY, January 7-28, 1967; LAING ART GALLERY, Newcastle, February 4-25; GRAVES ART GALLERY, Sheffield, March 4-25; reserved for Scotland, April 1-22.

WHITECHAPEL GALLERY, London, June-July, 1966, *The New Generation: 1966.* Preface by Bryan Robertson; Introduction by Robert Hughes.

GALLERY FRIEDRICH-DAHLEM, Munich, October-November, 1966, *British Sculpture.*

CAMDEN ARTS CENTRE, London, October, 1966, *New Dimensions.* An exhibition organized by the Hampstead Artists Council. Introduction by Eddie Worfram.

# UNITED STATES

## Books and articles

ASHTON, DORE. "La Sculpture Américaine", *XXe Siècle*, Paris vol. XXII, no. 15, December, 1960, pp. 85-91.

"New Talent USA: Sculpture, (Chosen by J.I.H. Baur, D.C. Miller, & D.G. Seckler)", *Art in America*, New York, vol. 49, no. 1, 1961, pp. 34-35.

"New Talent USA: Sculpture, (Chosen by Robert Scull)", *Art in America*, New York, vol. 50, no. 1, Spring 1962, pp. 32-39.

COPLANS, JOHN. "California Sculpture Today", *Artforum*, San Francisco, vol. II, no. 2, August, 1963, pp. 3-6.

LUCAS, J. "In the Wake of a Brazen Hussy: American Sculptors in Rome Today", *Arts*, New York, vol. 38, no. 1, October, 1963, pp. 18-22.

KOZLOFF, MAX. "American Sculpture in Transition", *Arts*, New York, vol. 38, no. 9, May, 1964, pp. 19-25.

FULLER, MARY. "San Francisco Sculptors", *Art in America*, New York, vol. 52, no. 3, June, 1964, pp. 52-56.

AGOSTINI, PETER; MALLARY, ROBERT; FRIEDMAN, MARTIN. "Is Sculpture a Step-child? A Colloquy", *Art News*, New York, vol. 63, no. 5, September, 1964, pp. 40-42+.

MONTE, JAMES D. "Bay Area Polychrome Sculpture", *Artforum*, San Francisco, vol. III, no. 2, November, 1964, pp. 40-43.

ROSE, BARBARA. "Looking at American Sculpture", *Artforum*, San Francisco, vol. III, no. 5, February, 1965, pp. 29-39.

KOZLOFF, MAX. "The Further Adventures of American Sculpture", *Arts*, New York, vol. 39, no. 5, February, 1965, pp. 24-31.

LIPPARD, LUCY R. "The Third Stream: Constructed Paintings and Painted Structures", *Art Voices*, New York, vol. 4, no. 2, Spring 1965, pp. 44-49.

*It Is*, New York, Special Issue #6, "Waldorf Panels 1 & 2 on Sculpture", Autumn 1965.

ROSE, BARBARA. "ABC Art", *Art in America*, New York, vol. 53, no. 3, October-November, 1965, pp. 57-69.

CUMMINGS, PAUL. *A Dictionary of American Artists*, New York, St. Martin's Press, 1966.

BOURDON, DAVID. "E=Mc² a Go-Go", *Art News*, New York, vol. 64, no. 9, January, 1966, pp. 22-25+.

MORRIS, ROBERT. "Notes on Sculpture", *Artforum*, Los Angeles, vol. IV, no. 6, February, 1966, pp. 42-44; "Notes on Sculpture, part II", *Artforum*, vol. V, no. 2, October, 1966, pp. 20-23; "Notes on Sculpture, part III", *Artforum*, vol. V, no. 10, Summer 1967, pp. 24-29.

LIPPARD, LUCY R. "New York Letter: Recent Sculpture as Escape", *Art International*, Zurich, vol. X, no. 2, February 20, 1966, pp. 48-58.

BOCHNER, M. "Primary Structures", *Arts*, New York, vol. 40, no. 8, June, 1966, pp. 32-35.

SMITHSON, ROBERT. "The New Moments and Entropy", *Artforum*, Los Angeles, vol. IV, no. 10, June, 1966, pp. 26-31.

HUTCHINSON, PETER. "Mannerism in the Abstract", *Art and Artists*, London, vol. 1, no. 6, September, 1966, pp. 18-21.

ROBINS, CORINNE. "Object, Structure or Sculpture: Where are we?", *Arts*, New York, vol. 40, no. 9, September-October, 1966, pp. 33-37.

LIPPARD, LUCY. "Rejective Art", *Art International*, Lugano, vol. X, no. 8, October 20, 1966, pp. 33-36.

FRIED, MICHAEL. "Art and Objecthood", *Artform*, New York, vol. V, no. 10, Summer 1967, pp. 12-23.

ANDERSEN, WAYNE. "American Sculpture: The Situation in the Fifties", *Artforum*, New York, vol. V, no. 10, Summer 1967, pp. 60-67.

## Exhibitions

*Recent Sculpture U.S.A.* An exhibition organized by the Junior Council of the Museum of Modern Art, New York. Introduction by James Thrall Soby and Walter Bareiss. Circulated to LOS ANGELES COUNTY MUSEUM, February 22-April 3, 1960; CITY ART MUSEUM OF ST. LOUIS, May 3-June 12, 1960; MUSEUM OF FINE ARTS, Boston, September 14-October 16, 1960.

STABLE GALLERY, New York, September 27-October 15, 1960, *New Sculpture Group: Fifth Exhibition*.

GALERIE CLAUDE BERNARD, Paris, October, 1960, *Sculpture Americaine*.

GALERIE CHALETTE, New York, December, 1960-January, 1961, *Structure and Sculpture*. Text by Mario Salvadori.

WHITNEY MUSEUM OF AMERICAN ART, New York, December 7, 1960-January 22, 1961, *Annual Exhibition 1960, Contemporary Sculpture and Drawings*.

KRANNERT ART MUSEUM, University of Illinois, Urbana, Illinois, February 26-April 2, 1961, *Contemporary American Painting and Sculpture*.

STABLE GALLERY, New York, September 19-October 14, 1961, *New Sculpture Group: Sixth Exhibition*.

THE ART INSTITUTE OF CHICAGO, Chicago, January 5-February 18, 1962, *65th Annual American Exhibition: Some Directions in Contemporary Painting and Sculpture*.

WHITNEY MUSEUM OF AMERICAN ART, New York, March 20-May 13, 1962, *Geometric Abstraction in America*.

THE RIVERSIDE MUSEUM, New York, April 8-29, 1962, *12 New York Sculptors*.

THE GEORGE PEABODY COLLEGE FOR TEACHERS, Nashville, Tennessee, October 15-December 1, 1962, *American Sculpture 1962-1963*. Text by Sidney Geist. Circulated to THE UNIVERSITY OF TENNESSEE, Knoxville, January 2-February 8, 1963; HENDRIX COLLEGE, Arkansas, February 22-March 30, 1963; UNIVERSITY OF ALABAMA, Tuscaloosa, April 12-May 17, 1963.

WHITNEY MUSEUM OF AMERICAN ART, New York, October 23-December 2, 1962, *Fifty California Artists*. An exhibition organized by the San Francisco Museum of Art with the assistance of the Los Angeles County Museum of Art. Circulated to WALKER ART CENTER, Minneapolis, February 17-March 17, 1963; ALBRIGHT-KNOX ART GALLERY, Buffalo, April 10-May 8, 1963; DES MOINES ART CENTER, May 24-June 23, 1963.

THE NEW SCHOOL ART CENTER, New School for Social Research, New York, November 6-28, 1962, *Humanities of the 60's; Man in Modern Sculpture, Drawing and Print*. Text by Paul Moscanyi.

WHITNEY MUSEUM OF AMERICAN ART, New York, December 12, 1962-February 3, 1963, *Annual Exhibition 1962, Contemporary Sculpture and Drawings*.

THE ART INSTITUTE OF CHICAGO, Chicago, January 11-February 10, 1963, *66th Annual American Exhibition: Directions in Contemporary Painting and Sculpture*.

PASADENA ART MUSEUM, Pasadena, California, February 11-March 7, 1964, *New American Sculpture*.

UNIVERSITY ART GALLERY, University of California at Berkeley, February 15-March 25, 1964, *Onze Sculpteurs Américains* (from the Biennale de Paris, 1963).

THE ART INSTITUTE OF CHICAGO, Chicago, February 28-April 12, 1964, *67th Annual American Exhibition: Directions in Contemporary Painting and Sculpture*.

KRANNERT ART MUSEUM, University of Illinois, Urbana, Illinois, March 3-April 7, 1963, *Contemporary American Painting and Sculpture—Eleventh Exhibition*.

WADSWORTH ATHENEUM, Hartford, Connecticut, July 18-September 15, 1963, *Eleven New England Sculptors*.

HOWARD WISE GALLERY, New York, March 5-28, 1964, *The Ten U.S.A. Sculptors of the 1963 São Paulo Bienal*.

DE CORDOVA MUSEUM, Lincoln, Massachusetts, June 14-September 20, 1964, *New England Art in 6 Parts: Part 4: Sculpture*.

STEDELIJK MUSEUM, Amsterdam, June 22-July 26, 1964, *De Niewe Americaanse Kunst* (American Pop Art). Text by Alan Solomon.

WHITNEY MUSEUM OF AMERICAN ART, New York, June 24-September 23, 1964, *Between the Fairs: 25 Years of American Art, 1939-1964*.

THE JEWISH MUSEUM, New York, October 15-November 29, 1964, *Recent American Sculpture*. Text by Hans van Weeren Griek.

SMITH COLLEGE MUSEUM OF ART, Northampton, Massachusetts, November 19-December 16, 1964, *Sight-Sound*.

WHITNEY MUSEUM OF AMERICAN ART, New York, December 9, 1964-January 31, 1965, *Annual Exhibit 1964: Contemporary American Sculpture*.

THE GEORGE PEABODY COLLEGE FOR TEACHERS, Nashville, Tennessee, May 3-28, 1965, *Sculpture 1965*. Text by Edward Bleicher. First exhibited at JOE AND EMILY LOWE GALLERY, University of Miami, Coral Gables, Florida, January 3-22, 1965. Circulated to UNIVERSITY OF TENNESSEE, Knoxville, February 7-26, 1965; UNIVERSITY OF KENTUCKY, Lexington, Kentucky, March 28-April 18, 1965.

WHITNEY MUSEUM OF AMERICAN ART, New York, June 23-August 29, 1965, *Young America 1965, Thirty American Artists Under Thirty-Five*. Text by Lloyd Goodrich.

KRANNERT ART MUSEUM, University of Illinois, Urbana, Illinois, March 7-April 11, 1965, *Twelfth Exhibition of Contemporary American Painting and Sculpture*.

LOEB ART CENTER, New York University, New York, April 6-29, 1965, *Concrete Expressionism*. Texts by Ruth Gurin, Irving Sandler.

AMERICAN EXPRESS PAVILION, NEW YORK WORLD'S FAIR, New York, 1965, *Art '65, Lesser Known and Unknown Painters; Young American Sculpture East to West*. Text on Sculpture by Wayne Andersen.

WHITNEY MUSEUM OF AMERICAN ART, New York, April 20-May 15, 1965. *Contemporary American Sculpture: Sculpture Selection 1.* Assembled by The Howard and Jean Lipman Foundation and the Whitney Museum of American Art.

MUSÉE RODIN, Paris, June 22-October 10, 1965, *États-Unis: Sculptures du XXe Siècle.* Texts by Cécile Goldscheider, René d'Harnoncourt. Traveling exhibition organized by the International Council of the Museum of Modern Art, New York, circulated to HOCHSCHULE FÜR BILDENDE KÜNSTE, Berlin, November 20, 1965-January 9, 1966, STAATLICHE KUNSTHALLE, Baden-Baden, February 25-April 17, 1966.

INSTITUTE OF CONTEMPORARY ART, University of Pennsylvania, Philadelphia, December, 1965-January 17, 1966, *7 Sculptors.*

ART GALLERY OF THE UNIVERSITY OF CALIFORNIA, Irvine, California, January 7-February 6, 1966, *Five Los Angeles Sculptors.* Text by John Coplans.

THE JEWISH MUSEUM, New York, April 27-June 12, 1966, *Primary Structures: Younger American and British Sculptors.* Text by Kynaston McShine.

FINCH COLLEGE MUSEUM OF ART, New York, May 11-June 30, 1966, *Art in Process: The Visual Development of Structure.*

LA JOLLA MUSEUM OF ART, La Jolla, California, May 20-June 26, 1966, *New Modes in California Painting and Sculpture.* Text by Donald J. Brewer.

THE ART INSTITUTE OF CHICAGO, Chicago, August 19-October 16, 1966, *68th Annual American Exhibition.*

THE NELSON GALLERY AND ATKINS MUSEUM, Kansas City, Missouri, November 4-December 4, 1966, *Sound, Light, Silence: Art that Performs.*

WHITNEY MUSEUM OF AMERICAN ART, New York, December 16, 1966-February 5, 1967, *Annual Exhibition 1966, Contemporary Sculpture and Prints.*

WALKER ART CENTER, Minneapolis, October 22- December 4, 1966, *Eight Sculptors: The Ambiguous Image.* Texts by Martin Friedman, Jan van der Marck.

LOS ANGELES COUNTY MUSEUM OF ART, Los Angeles, April 28-June 25, 1967, *American Sculpture of the Sixties.* Maurice Tuchman, ed. Texts by Lawrence Alloway, Wayne Andersen, Dore Ashton, Clement Greenberg, Max Kozloff, Lucy L. Lippard, James Monte, Barbara Rose, Irving Sandler. Circulated to PHILADELPHIA MUSEUM OF ART, Philadelphia, September 15-October 29, 1967.

THE WASHINGTON GALLERY OF MODERN ART, Washington, D.C., May 6-June 25, 1967, *A New Aesthetic.* Text by Barbara Rose.

FINCH COLLEGE MUSEUM OF ART, New York, May 12-June 8, 1967, *Schemata 7.* Text and interviews with artists by Elayne H. Varian.


# YUGOSLAVIA

## Books and Articles

KOLARIĆ, MIODRAG. *Novija Jugoslovenska Skulptura,* Belgrade, 1961.

MARKUS, ZORAN. "La Sculpture Yougoslave Contemporaine", *Syntheses,* Brussels, no. 223, December 1964.

HORVAT-PINTARIĆ, VERA. "Suvremena Jugoslavenska Umjetnost", *Civiltà delle Macchine,* Rome, no. 3, May-June 1964, pp. 33-40.

## Exhibitions

MODERNA GALERIJA, Ljubljana, Yugoslavia, November, 1961. *Premio Morgan's Paint: III mednarodni biennale slikarstva in kiparstva.* Texts by Francesco Arcangeli, Zoran Kržišnik, Eugenio Riccomini.

STÄTISCHES MUSEUM / GEMÄLDEGALERIE, Wiesbaden, Germany, March 25-May 28, 1961, *Neue Jugoslawische Kunst.* Text by Zoran Kržišnik.

TATE GALLERY, London, April 28-May 28, 1961, *Contemporary Yugoslav Painting and Sculpture.* Text by Zoran Kržišnik, Drago Vucinic. Exhibit organized by The Arts Council of Great Britain. Circulated to HERBERT ART GALLERY, Coventry, June 17-July 8, 1961; FERENS ART GALLERY, Kingston-Upon-Hull, July 15-August 5, 1961; BRIGHTON ART GALLERY, Brighton, August 12-September 3, 1961.

MUSÉE NATIONAL D'ART MODERNE, Paris, December 20, 1961-January 28, 1962, *L'Art Contemporain en Yougoslavie.*

PALAZZO DELLA ESPOSIZIONI, Rome, May-June, 1962, *L'Arte Contemporanea in Jugoslavia.* Text by Zoran Kržišnik.

KÜNSTLERHAUS, Graz, Austria, September-October 1963, *Trigon '63.*

STÄDTISCHE KUNSTGALERIE, Bochum, Germany, September 17-October 10, 1966, *Profile VI: Jugoslawische Kunst Heute.* Text by Zoran Kržišnik.

THE CORCORAN GALLERY, Washington, D.C., January 7-February 13, 1966, *Yugoslavia/Contemporary Trends/The Younger Generation.*

# III. BIBLIOGRAPHY AND EXHIBITIONS BY ARTIST

In each case the most recent major reference is listed first. Entries which follow include one-man exhibitions, important international group exhibitions, and principal bibliographical items subsequent in date to the original reference. In certain cases important references which had been omitted in the original reference have also been listed.

## PETER AGOSTINI

For bibliography and exhibition list see:
THE JEWISH MUSEUM, New York, October 15-November 29, 1964, *Recent American Sculpture*. Text on Agostini by Max Kozloff.

### One-man exhibitions

GALERIE GRIMAUD, New York, February-March 22, 1959.
STEPHEN RADICH GALLERY, New York, November 15-December 10, 1960.
STEPHEN RADICH GALLERY, New York, May 8-June 2, 1962. *Agostini: Sculpture and Drawings.*
STEPHEN RADICH GALLERY, New York, April 9-May 4, 1963.
STEPHEN RADICH GALLERY, New York, November 3-28, 1964.
STEPHEN RADICH GALLERY, New York, January 11-February 12, 1966.

### Selected group exhibitions

LOS ANGELES COUNTY MUSEUM OF ART, Los Angeles, April 28-June 25, 1967, *American Sculpture of the Sixties*. (Hereafter listed as LOS ANGELES COUNTY MUSEUM OF ART, Los Angeles, 1967).

## KENNETH ARMITAGE

For bibliography and exhibition list see:
LYNTON, NORBERT. *Kenneth Armitage*, London, Methuen, 1962.

### One-man exhibitions

GALERIJA GRADA ZAGREBA, Zagreb, February 26-March 14, 1962. Text by Vera Horvat-Pintarić.
PAUL ROSENBERG AND CO., New York, March 6-31, 1963.
MARLBOROUGH NEW LONDON GALLERY, LONDON, May, 1962.
GALERIE CHARLES LIENHARD, Zurich, June 18-July, 1963. Text by Alan Bowness.
MARLBOROUGH NEW LONDON GALLERY, London, April, 1965.

### Selected group exhibitions

DOCUMENTA III, Kassel, Germany, June 27-October 5, 1964, *Malerei und Skulptur*.
EXPO 67, Montreal, Canada, April-October, 1967, *International Exhibition of Contemporary Sculpture*.

### Bibliography

BOWNESS, ALAN. "Recent Sculpture of Kenneth Armitage", *Motif II*, Summer 1963.
RUSSELL, J. "Armitage by TKO", *Art News*, New York, vol. 64, no. 4, Summer 1965, p. 49+.

## JEAN (HANS) ARP

For bibliography see:
SOBY JAMES THRALL, *Arp*, New York, Museum of Modern Art, 1958.
MARCHIORI, GIUSEPPE, *Arp*, Milan, Bruno Alfieri, 1964.

### One-man exhibitions

MUSEUM FOLKWANG, Essen, 1959. Circulated to STÄDTLICHE KUNSTHALLE, Mannheim; KUNSTVEREIN, Hamburg; STAATLICHE KUNSTHALLE, Baden-Baden, 1959-60.
STEDELIJK MUSEUM, Amsterdam, 1960.
GALERIE DENISE RENÉ, Paris, June-July, 1960, *Arp, Sculptures et Tapisseries Récentes*.
GALERIE CHALETTE, New York, October-November, 1960. Text, "The Spiritual Mission of Art" by Michel Seuphor.
SIDNEY JANIS GALLERY, New York, 1960.
KLIPSTEIN UND KORNFELD, Bern, January 11-February 24, 1962, *Hans Arp Zeichnungen und Collagen, Papiers Déchirés und Reliefs*.

MUSÉE NATIONAL D'ART MODERNE, Paris, February 21-April 21, 1962. Text by Jean Cassou. Circulated to TATE GALLERY, London, November 24-December 23, 1962. Text by Alan Bowness.
GALERIE DU PERRON, Geneva, June 15-September 1, 1962, *Hommage à Jean Arp*.
MODERNA MUSEET, Stockholm, August-September, 1962.
GALERIE RENÉE ZIEGLER, Zurich, September 27-October 20, 1962.
NEW ART CENTER GALLERY, New York, November 3-30, 1962.
BORGENICHT GALLERY, New York, November, 1962.
EVERETT ELLIN GALLERY, Los Angeles, March 25-April 13, 1963.
SIDNEY JANIS GALLERY, New York, April 29-May 25, 1963.
GALLERIA SCHWARZ, Milan, November 30-December 31, 1963.
GALLERIA LA LOGGIA, Bologna, January 16-February 12, 1964.
BROOK STREET GALLERY, London, May 19-Summer, 1964.
GALERIE CHALETTE, New York, January-February, 1965. Text by Hans Richter.
PACE GALLERY, Boston, February 13-March 13, 1965.
GALLERIA SCHWARZ, Milan, May 8-June 4, 1965. Text, "For Arp, Art is Arp" by Marcel Duchamp.
GALLERIA FLAVIANA, Locarno, May 21-August, 1966.
WÜRTTEMBERGISCHER KUNSTVEREIN, Stuttgart, September 16-October 23, 1966.
GALERIE IM ERKER, St. Gallen, Switzerland, November 5, 1966-January 31, 1967. Text by Jean Cassou, Max Hölzer, Arp and others.
GEMEENTE MUSEUM, The Hague, February 18-April 16, 1967.

### Selected group exhibitions

DOCUMENTA II, Kassel, Germany, July 11-October 11, 1959.
XXXI BIENNALE INTERNAZIONALE D'ARTE VENEZIA, Venice, June 16-October 7, 1962.
DOCUMENTA III, Kassel, Germany, June 27-October 5, 1964.
VIII BIENAL DE SÃO PAULO, São Paulo, Brazil, September-November, 1965.
EXPO 67, Montreal, Canada, April-October, 1967, *International Exhibition of Contemporary Sculpture*.

### Bibliography

GIEDION-WELCKER, CAROLA. "Die Welt der Formen und Phantome bei Hans Arp", *Quadrum*, Brussels, no. 11, 1961, pp. 19-46+.
CHEVALIER, DENYS. "Jean Arp", *Aujourd'hui*, Boulogne-sur-Seine, vol. 6, no. 36, April, 1962, pp. 4-7.
VERDET, ANDRÉ, "La rétrospective de Arp au Musée national d'art moderne", *XXe Siècle*, Paris, vol. 24, no. 19, June, 1962, pp. 100-106.
SEUPHOR, MICHEL. "Arcadie d'Arp", *XXe Siècle*, Paris, vol. 24, no. 19, June, 1962, pp. 26-29.
GIEDION-WELCKER, CAROLA. "Zu Hans Arp's Spätwerk", *Werk*, Winterthur, vol. 50, no. 4, April, 1963, pp. 52-60.
HUELSENBECK, RICHARD. "Hans Arp", *Kunstwerk*, Baden-Baden, vol. 20, nos. 1-2, October-November, 1966, pp. 84-86.

## LARRY BELL

For bibliography and exhibition list see:
LOS ANGELES COUNTY MUSEUM OF ART, Los Angeles, 1967.

### One-man exhibition

PACE GALLERY, New York, April 20-May 27, 1967.

### Selected group exhibitions

THE WASHINGTON GALLERY OF MODERN ART, Washington, D.C., May 6-June 25, 1967, *A New Aesthetic*. Text by Barbara Rose.

### Bibliography

DANIELI, FIDEL A. "Bell's Progress", *Artforum*, New York, vol. V, no. 10, Summer 1967, pp. 68-71.

## MAX BILL

For bibliography and exhibition list see:
GALERIE IM ERKER, St. Gallen, Switzerland, April 8-May 27, 1967, *Max Bill*. Texts by Will Grohmann, Max Bense, Max Bill.

### Selected group exhibition

EXPO 67, Montreal, Canada, April-October, 1967, *International Exhibition of Contemporary Sculpture.*

### Bibliography

GOMRINGER, EUGEN. "Max Bill: Vielfalt und Einheit der gestalteten Welt", *Werk*, Winterthur, vol. 47, no. 8, August, 1960, pp. 289-291.
STABER, MARGIT. "Max Bill und die Umweltgestaltung", *Zodiac*, Milan, no. 9, 1962, pp. 60-95.
BENSE, MAX. "Max Bill 1963", *Art International*, Lugano, vol. VIII, no. 3, March 25, 1963, pp. 30-35.
BORGHERO, E. "L'Esposizione nazionale svizzera, Losanna 1964", *L'Architettura*, Milan, vol. 10, September, 1964, pp. 304-305.
KINSMAN, R.D. "Search for Truth", *Detroit Institute of Arts Bulletin*, Detroit, vol. 43, 1964, pp. 3-7.
HILL, ANTHONY. "Constructivism, the European Phenomenon", *Studio International*, London, vol. 171, no. 876, April, 1966, pp. 140-147.

## RONALD BLADEN

For bibliography and exhibition list see:
LOS ANGELES COUNTY MUSEUM OF ART, Los Angeles, 1967.

### Selected group exhibitions

THE JEWISH MUSEUM, New York, April 27-June 12, 1966, *Primary Structures.*
EXPO '67, Montreal, Canada, April-October, 1967, *International Exhibition of Contemporary Sculpture.*

### Bibliography

HOLSTEIN, J. "New York's Vitality Tonic for Canadian Artists", *Canadian Art*, Ottawa, issue no. 93, vol. 21, no. 5, September, 1964, pp. 273-74.
BERKSON, WILLIAM. "Ronald Bladen: Sculpture and Where we Stand", *Art and Literature*, Lausanne, vol. 12, Spring 1967, pp. 139-150.

## POL BURY

For bibliography and exhibition list see:
TOSI, SERGIO. *Pol Bury*, Milan, André Balthazar, 1967.

### One-man exhibitions

KASMIN LTD., London, April, 1967.
J. D. HUDSON GALLERY, Detroit, May 3-27, 1967.

## ALEXANDER CALDER

For bibliography and exhibition list see:
LOS ANGELES COUNTY MUSEUM OF ART, Los Angeles, 1967.

### Selected group exhibitions

EXPO 67, Montreal, Canada, April-October, 1967, *International Exhibition of Contemporary Sculpture.*

## ANTHONY CARO

For bibliography and exhibition list see:
RIJKSMUSEUM KRÖLLER-MÜLLER, Otterlo, Holland, May 7-July 2, 1967, *Eduardo Paolozzi and Anthony Caro.* Caro text by Clement Greenberg.

### Selected group exhibitions

INSTITUTE OF CONTEMPORARY ART, University of Pennsylvania, Philadelphia, December, 1965-January 17, 1966, *7 Sculptors.* Caro text by Michael Benedikt.
LOS ANGELES COUNTY MUSEUM OF ART, Los Angeles, 1967.

### Bibliography

BARO, GENE. "A Look at Reminiscence", *Arts*, New York, vol. 38, no. 2, November, 1963, pp. 44-47.
RUSSELL, JOHN. "Portrait: Anthony Caro", *Art in America*, New York, vol. 54, no. 5, September-October, 1966, pp. 80-87.

## ANDREA CASCELLA

### One-man exhibitions

GALLERIA DELL'OBELISCO, Rome, 1949.
GALLERIA DEL CAVALLINO, Venice, 1951.
GALLERIA DEL MILANO, Milan, November 25-December 4, 1954.
GALLERIA DEL NAVIGLIO, Milan, 1956.
GALLERIA D'ARTE SELECTA, Rome, February 19-March 7, 1958, *Andrea e Pietro Cascella.* Poem by Michele Parrella.
GROSVENOR GALLERY, London, 1960.
GALLERIA DELL'ARIETE, Milan, June, 1961. Text by Emilio Tadini.
GROSVENOR GALLERY, London, June 6-July 7, 1962. Text by Marco Valsecchi.
GALLERIA DELL'ARIETE, Milan, November 15, 1963. Text by Emilio Tadini.
BETTY PARSONS GALLERY, New York, April 20-May 15, 1965. Text by Giuseppe Marchiori.
HOLLAND GALLERY, Chicago, 1967.

### Selected group exhibitions

XXV BIENNALE INTERNAZIONALE D'ARTE VENEZIA, Venice, 1950.
THE SOLOMON R. GUGGENHEIM MUSEUM, New York, October 3, 1962-January 6, 1963, *Modern Sculpture from the Joseph H. Hirshhorn Collection.*
XXXII BIENNALE INTERNAZIONALE D'ARTE VENEZIA, Venice, June 20-October 18, 1964. Text on Cascella by Marco Valsecchi.

### Bibliography

SCHÖENBERGER, GUALTIERO. "Andrea Cascella", *Art International*, Lugano, vol. VII, no. 3, March 25, 1963, pp. 61-64.
RUSSOLI, FRANCO. "Andrea Cascella", *Quadrum*, Brussels, no. 14, 1963, pp. 138-139.
F. M., "Andrea Cascella", *Domus*, Milan, no. 412, March, 1964, pp. 35-38.
DORFLES, GILLO. "Andrea Cascella, Unitary Sculpture", *Studio International*, London, vol. 168, no. 860, December, 1964, pp. 250-255.
HOPE, J. "Andrea Cascella", *Architectural Review*, London, vol. CXLI, no. 840, February, 1967, p. 142.

## CÉSAR (BALDACCINI)

For bibliography and exhibition list see:
MUSÉE DES ARTS DÉCORATIFS, Paris, June-September, 1965, *Trois Sculpteurs: César, Roël D'Haese, Tinguely.* Text by François Mathey.

### One-man exhibitions

GALLERIA GALATEA, Turin, March 25-April 20, 1966. Text by Luigi Carluccio.
STEDELIJK MUSEUM, Amsterdam, May 13-June 26, 1966.
MUSEUM CANTINI, Marseille, October-November, 1966. Texts by François Mathey and Douglas Cooper.
GALERIE MADOURA, Cannes, 1966. Text by Douglas Cooper.

### Selected group exhibitions

EXPO 67, Montreal, Canada, April-October, 1967, *International Exhibition of Contemporary Sculpture.*

### Bibliography

SELZ, P. "Nouvelles images de l'homme", *L'Oeil*, Paris, no. 62, February, 1960, pp. 47-53.
RUSSELL, J. "César", *Art News*, New York, vol. 59, no. 7, November, 1960, p. 25.
GIEDION-WELCKER, CAROLA. "Origines et tendances du relief", *XXe Siècle*, Paris, vol. XXIII, no. 16, May, 1961, pp. 3-15.
RUSSELL, J. "César à Londres", *XXe Siècle*, Paris, vol. XXIII, no. 16, May, 1961, (supplement).
GINDERTAEL, R. V. "Situations actuelles de la sculpture dans le cadre de l'Ecole de Paris", *Quadrum*, Brussels, no. 12, 1961, pp. 21-44.
RESTANY, P. "Le nouveau realisme und was darunter zu verstehen ist", *Kunstwerk*, Baden-Baden, vol. XVI, no. 7, January, 1963, (supplement).

# JOHN CHAMBERLAIN

For bibliography and exhibition list see:
LOS ANGELES COUNTY MUSEUM OF ART, Los Angeles, 1967.

## One-man exhibitions

LEO CASTELLI GALLERY, New York, January 13-February 3, 1962.
ROBERT FRASER GALLERY, London, May 14-June 8, 1963, *2 American Sculptors: Chamberlain, Stankiewicz.*
DWAN GALLERY, Los Angeles, November 29, 1966-January 7, 1967.

## Selected group exhibitions

XXXII BIENNALE INTERNAZIONALE D'ARTE VENEZIA, Venice, June 20-October 18, 1964.

# EDUARDO CHILLIDA

For exhibition list see:
THE MUSEUM OF FINE ARTS, Houston, October 4, 1966, *Eduardo Chillida.* Text by James Johnson Sweeney. Circulated to MUNSON-WILLIAMS-PROCTOR INSTITUTE, Utica, New York, January 15-February 12, 1967; CITY ART MUSEUM, St. Louis, March 9-April 15, 1967.

## One-man exhibition

GALERIE VÖMEL, Düsseldorf, March 15-April 30, 1967. Text by Werner Schmalenbach.

## Selected group exhibitions

EXPO 67, Montreal, Canada, April-October, 1967, *International Exhibition of Contemporary Sculpture.*

## Bibliography

LANES, JERROLD. "Spain in the Swim: A Series of Exhibitions in New York", *Arts*, New York, vol. 34, no. 10, September, 1960, p. 55.
NETTER, MARIA. "Der Baskische Bildhauer: Eduardo Chillida", *Werk*, Winterthur, vol. 49, no. 6, June, 1962, pp. 213-217.
SPENCER, C. S. "Chillida: Sculptor in Space", *Studio International*, London, vol. 169, no. 866, June, 1965, pp. 250-255.
ALVARD, JULIEN. "Artistes Espagnols de Paris: Chillida", *Aujourd'hui*, Boulogne-sur-Seine, vol. 9, no. 52, February, 1966, p. 67.
VOLBOUDT, PIERRE. *Eduardo Chillida*, London, Thames and Hudson, 1967. (in preparation).

# ETTORE COLLA

For bibliography and exhibition list see:
DELL'ARCO, MAURIZIO FAGIOLO. *Rapporto 60: Le Arti Oggi Italia*, Rome, Mario Bulzoni, editore, 1966.

## One-man exhibitions

GALLERIA LA SALITA, Rome, May, 1959. Texts by Charles Delloye and Emilio Villa. Circulated to INSTITUTE OF CONTEMPORARY ART, London, August-September, 1959; HATTON GALLERY, Durham University, Newcastle, December, 1959. Texts by Lawrence Alloway, Charles Delloye, Emilio Villa.
STEDELIJK MUSEUM, Amsterdam, April 1-May 2, 1960. Text (in supplement to catalogue) by G. C. Argan.

## Selected group exhibitions

MUSÉE RODIN, Paris, June-September, 1966, *3ème Exposition Internationale de Sculpture Contemporaine.*

## Bibliography

"Ettore Colla", *Domus*, Milan, no. 406, September, 1963, pp. 34-35, 59.
DELL'ARCO, MAURIZIO FAGIOLO. "Colla: Sculpture of the Iron Age", *Art International*, Lugano, Switzerland vol. XI, no. 5, May 20, 1967, pp. 18-21.

# PIETRO CONSAGRA

For exhibition list see:
MARLBOROUGH GALLERIA, Rome, December, 1966. *Consagra.* Text by Maurizio Calvesi.

## One-man exhibitions

PACE GALLERY, Boston, 1963. Text by Sam Hunter.
GALLERIA ODYSSIA, New York, January 5-30, 1965.
GALLERIA ODYSSIA, New York, March 15-April 15, 1966.
BOYMANS-VAN BEUNINGEN MUSEUM, Rotterdam, 1967.

## Selected group exhibitions

EXPO 67, Montreal, Canada, April-October, 1967, *International Exhibition of Contemporary Sculpture.*

## Bibliography

CONSAGRA, PIETRO. *La Necessità della Scultura*, Rome, Edizione Lentini, 1952.
MARCHIORI, G. *Scultura italiana moderna*, Venice, Alfieri, 1953.
APOLLONIO, U. *Pietro Consagra*, Rome, De Luca, 1956.
ARGAN, G. C. "Scultura di Consagra", *Quadrum*, Brussels, no. 2, 1956, pp. 139-144.
VENTURI, L. "Sculptures frontales de Consagra", *XXe Siécle*, Paris, vol. XXI, no. 13, 1960.
PONENTE, N. "Pietro Consagra", *Cimaise*, Paris, vol. 7, no. 50, October-November-December, 1960, pp. 96-104.
PONENTE, N. *Consagra*, Paris, Galerie de France, 1960.
CERNI, VICENTE AGUILERA, "Consideraziones Multiples de Pietro Consagra", *Correo de las Artes*, Barcelona, April, 1961.
ARGAN, G. C. "Pietro Consagra", *Art International*, Zurich, vol. VI, no. 2, 1962, pp. 54-56.
L.L.P. "I Ferri Colorati di Consagra", *Domus*, Milan, no. 443, October, 1966, pp. 43-44.

# WESSEL COUZIJN

For exhibition list see:
RIJKSMUSEUM, Amsterdam, November 10, 1966, *Couzijn: Uitreiking van de David Röellprijs aan Wessel Couzijn.* Text by A. M. Hammacher.

## Bibliography

SPENCER, C. S. "Wessel Couzijn and Pearl Pearlmutter", *Studio International*, London, vol. 166, no. 845, September, 1963, pp. 124-127.
HOFMANN, WERNER. "Wessel Couzijn", *Art International*, Lugano, vol. VII, no. 9, December 5, 1963, pp. 28-29.

# BURGOYNE DILLER

## One-man exhibitions

PINACOTHECA GALLERY, New York, to December 31, 1946.
PINACOTHECA GALLERY, New York, to December 30, 1949.
ROSE FRIED GALLERY, New York, to December 8, 1951.
GALERIE CHALETTE, New York, May, 1961, *Diller, Paintings, Constructions, Drawings, Watercolors.*
GALERIE CHALETTE, New York, March 7, 1964, *Color-Structures, Paintings and Drawings by Burgoyne Diller.*
THE NEW JERSEY STATE MUSEUM, Trenton, February 11-April 3, 1966, *Burgoyne Diller: 1906-1965.* Text by Lawrence Campbell (reprint from *Art News*, May, 1961.)

## Selected group exhibitions

MUSEUM OF ART, CARNEGIE INSTITUTE, Pittsburgh, October 30, 1964-January 10, 1965, *The 1964 Pittsburgh International Exhibition of Contemporary Painting and Sculpture.*

## Bibliography

DE KOONING, ELAINE. "Diller Paints a Picture", *Art News*, New York, vol. 51, no. 9, January, 1953, pp. 26-29.
CAMPBELL, LAWRENCE. "Rule that Measures Emotion", *Art News*, New York, vol. 60, no. 3, May, 1961, pp. 34-35.
TILLIM, SIDNEY. "Month in Review", *Arts*, New York, vol. 35, no. 8, May-June, 1961, pp. 78-81.

## MARK DI SUVERO

For bibliography and exhibition list see:
LOS ANGELES COUNTY MUSEUM OF ART, Los Angeles, 1967.

### Bibliography

ROSENSTEIN, HARRIS. "Di Suvero: the pressures of reality", *Art News*, New York, vol. 65, no. 10, February, 1967, pp. 36-39.
KOZLOFF, MAX. "Mark Di Suvero: Leviathan", *Artforum*, New York, vol. V, no. 10, Summer 1967, pp. 41-46.

## ÉTIENNE-MARTIN

For bibliography and exhibition list see:
MUSÉE D'ART ET D'INDUSTRIE DE SAINT-ÉTIENNE, Saint-Etienne, France, 1966. Text by Jean Dypréau.

### Selected group exhibitions

EXPO 67, Montreal, Canada, April-October, 1967, *International Exhibition of Contemporary Sculpture.*

### Bibliography

JOUFFROY, A. "Portrait d'un artiste: Étienne-Martin", *Arts, Spectacles*, Paris, no. 554, February 8-14, 1956.
GINDERTAEL, R. V., "Le Grand oeuvre d'Étienne-Martin", *Quadrum*, Brussels, no. 19, 1965, pp. 67-78.

## LUCIO FONTANA

For bibliography and exhibition list see:
WALKER ART CENTER, Minneapolis, Minnesota, January 6-February 13, 1966, *Lucio Fontana: The Spatial Concept of Art.* Texts by Jan van der Marck, Arman, Otto Piene.

### One-man exhibitions

GALERIE ALEXANDRE IOLAS, Paris, March 23-April 23, 1966.
CENTRO DE ARTES VISUALES DEL INSTITUTO TORCUATO DI TELLA, Buenos Aires, July 26-August 18, 1966.
MARLBOROUGH-GERSON GALLERY, New York, January 20-February 18, 1967.
STEDELIJK MUSEUM, Amsterdam, March 23-May 7, 1967.

### Selected group exhibitions

XXXIII BIENNALE INTERNAZIONALE D'ARTE VENEZIA, Venice, June 18-October 16, 1966.

### Bibliography

HOCTIN, L. "Les Ballons de Lucio Fontana", *XXe Siècle*, Paris, vol. XXIII, no. 16, May, 1961, (supplement).
LEONHARD, K. "Lucio Fontana", *Kunstwerk*, Baden-Baden, vol. 15, nos. 1-2, July, 1961, pp. 14-26.
MORUCCHIO, B. "Lucio Fontana, pour une nouvelle synthèse des arts", *Aujourd'hui*, Boulogne-sur-Seine, vol. 6, no. 36, April, 1962, pp. 14-15.
CIRLOT, JUAN EDUARDO. *Lucio Fontana*, Barcelona, Gustavo Gili, 1966.
DELL'ARCO, MAURIZIO FAGIOLO. *Rapporto 60: Le Arti Oggi Italia*, Rome, Mario Bolzoni, editore, 1966.
PONENTE, NELLO. "Continuità di Fontana", *La Biennale di Venezia*, Venice, vol. XVI, no. 60, December, 1966, pp. 10-19.

## NORIYASU FUKUSHIMA

### One-man exhibition

GALERIE 16, Kyoto, 1966.

### Selected group exhibitions

NATIONAL MUSEUM OF MODERN ART, Kyoto, April 4-May 10, 1964, *Contemporary Trend of Japanese Paintings and Sculptures.*
9TH INTERNATIONAL BIENNALE EXHIBITION IN TOKYO, Tokyo, 1967.

## ALBERTO GIACOMETTI

For bibliography see:
THE MUSEUM OF MODERN ART, New York, June 9-October 10, 1965, *Alberto Giacometti.* Texts by Peter Selz and Alberto Giacometti. Circulated to THE ART INSTITUTE OF CHICAGO, November 5-December 12, 1965; LOS ANGELES COUNTY MUSEUM OF ART, January 11-February 20, 1966; SAN FRANCISCO MUSEUM OF ART, March 10-April 24, 1966.
For exhibition list see:
KUNSTHALLE, Basel, June 25-August 28, 1966, *Giacometti.*

### One-man exhibitions

WORLD HOUSE GALLERIES, New York, January 12-February 6, 1960.
THE PHILLIPS COLLECTION, Washington, D.C., February 2-March 4, 1963. Text by Duncan Phillips.
LOUISIANA MUSEUM, Humlebaek, Denmark, September 18-October 24, 1965, (modified version of Tate Gallery exhibition).

### Bibliography

"Alberto Giacometti", *Derrière le Miroir*, Paris, no. 127, May, 1961. Texts by O. Larronde, L. Leclercq, Isaku Yanaihara.
MATTER, M. "Giacometti: in the vicinity of the Impossible," *Art News*, New York, vol. 64, no. 4, Summer 1965, pp. 26-31+.
LORD, J. *A Giacometti Portrait*, New York, The Museum of Modern Art, 1965.
"Brief An Pierre Matisse", *Kunstwerk*, Baden-Baden, vol. XIX, no. 7, January, 1966, pp. 14-17.
CAMPBELL, R. "Alberto Giacometti 1901-1966, a personal Reminiscence," *Studio International*, London, vol. 171, no. 874, February, 1966, p. 47.
LORD, J. "In Memorium Alberto Giacometti," *L'Oeil*, Paris, no. 135, March, 1966, pp. 42-46+.
SAN LAZZARO. "Giacometti," *XXe Siècle*, Paris, vol. XXVIII, no. 26, May, 1966 (supplement).
AMMANN, J.C. "Das Problem des Raumes im werk Alberto Giacomettis," *Werk*, Winterthur, vol. 53, no. 6, June, 1966, pp. 237-240.
MATTER, M. "Giacometti," *Life*, New York, January 28, 1966, pp. 53-60.
GIEDION-WELCKER, C. "Alberto Giacometti auf siener Suche nach Wahrheit," *Kunstwerk*, Baden-Baden, vol. XX, nos. 1-2, October, 1966, pp. 4-12.

## GÜNTER HAESE

For bibliography and exhibition list see:
MARLBOROUGH FINE ART LTD., London, November-December, 1965, *Günter Haese.* Text by Herbert Pée.

### Selected group exhibitions

XXXIII BIENNALE INTERNAZIONALE D'ARTE VENEZIA, Venice, June 18-October 16, 1966.

### Bibliography

"Günter Haese's Clockworks," *Horizon*, New York, vol. IX, no. 3, Summer 1967, pp. 62-63.

## ROËL D'HAESE

For bibliography and exhibition list see:
MUSÉE DES ARTS DÉCORATIFS, Paris, June-September, 1965, *Trois Sculpteurs: César, Roël D'Haese, Tinguely.* Text by Chris Yperman.

### Bibliography

DYPRÉAU, J. "Roël d'Haese ou l'angoisse apprivoisée", *XXe Siècle*, Paris, vol. XXVI, no. 23, May, 1964, pp. 59-63.
"Le Chant du Mal de Roël d'Haese", *Quadrum*, Brussels, no. 17, 1964, pp. 156-157.

# BARBARA HEPWORTH

For bibliography see:
HODIN, DR. J. P. *Barbara Hepworth*, London, Lund Humphries Ltd., 1961.
For exhibition list see:
GIMPEL FILS, London, May-June, 1966, *Barbara Hepworth*.

## One-man exhibition

MODERNA MUSEET, Stockholm, November-December, 1964. Text by J. P. Hodin.

## Selected group exhibitions

EXPO 67, Montreal, Canada, April-October, 1967, *International Exhibition of Contemporary Sculpture*.

## Bibliography

HODIN, J. P. "Artist and Architect: recent Monumental Works produced in England," *Quadrum*, Brussels, no. 10, 1961, pp. 24-26.
LEVY, M. "Impulse and rhythm: Barbara Hepworth," *Studio International*, London, vol. 164, no. 833, September, 1962, pp. 84-91.
HODIN, J. P. "Barbara Hepworth et la tradition classique," *XXe Siècle*, Paris, vol. XXVII, no. 25, June, 1965, pp. 100-104.
BARO, G. "Barbara Hepworth in her times," *Studio International*, London, vol. 171, no. 878, June, 1966, pp. 252-257.

# RUDOLF HOFLEHNER

For bibliography and exhibition list see:
HAUS AM WALDSEE, Berlin, March 10-May 7, 1967, *Rudolf Hoflehner*. Text by Kristian Sotriffer. Also shown at STÄDTISCHES MUSEUM, Leverkusen, May 26-July 2, 1967.

## Bibliography

MAUER, OTTO. "Rudolf Hoflehner," *Musée Labyrinthe*, Aschaffenburg, Germany, no. 1, January, 1963, pp. 23-28.

# MASAKAZU HORIUTI

## One-man exhibitions

KAMAKURA MUSEUM OF MODERN ART, Kamakura, 1963-64.
KYOTO MUNICIPAL MUSEUM OF ART, Kyoto, May 21-June 18, 1966.
AKIYAMA GALLERY, Tokyo, January 10-16, 1967.
GALERIE 16, Kyoto, April 3-9, 1967.

## Bibliography

HOMMA, MASAYOCHI. "Conversation in the Studio", *Art Notes*, Tokyo, no. 6, 1963, p. 53. Text in Japanese.

# JEAN IPOUSTEGUY

For bibliography and exhibition list see:
STÄDTISCHES MUSEUM, Leverkusen, December 12, 1966-January 1, 1967, *Ipousteguy*. Texts by Jürgen Claus, Dagobert Frey, Ipousteguy.

## One-man exhibitions

WÜRTTEMBERGISCHER KUNSTVEREIN, Stuttgart, March 25-April 24, 1966.
GALERIE CLAUDE BERNARD, Paris, November 8-December, 1966. Text by Walter Lewino.

## Selected group exhibitions

EXPO 67, Montreal, Canada, April-October, 1967, *International Exhibition of Contemporary Sculpture*.

## Bibliography

LASSAIGNE, J. "Ipousteguy", *Studio International*, London, vol. 169, no. 865, May, 1965, pp. 200-203.

# ROBERT JACOBSEN

For bibliography and exhibition list see:
GALERIE DE FRANCE, Paris, April 23-May 18, 1963, *Jacobsen: Sculptures 1961-1962*. Text by Pierre Descarques.

## One-man exhibitions

GALERIE DE FRANCE, Paris, November 12-December 12, 1958.
GALERIE BIRCH, Copenhagen, March 5, 1959. Text by Jean Laude.
STEDELIJK MUSEUM, Amsterdam, March, 1960, Text by Eugene Ionesco.
KUNSTNERNES KUNSTHANDEL, Copenhagen and GUMMERSONS KONST-GALLERI, Stockholm, 1961. Text by Kristian Romare.
KOOTZ GALLERY, New York, February 13-March 3, 1962, *Sculpture by Jacobsen*.
GALERIE HYBLER, Copenhagen, 1963. Text by Ejner Johannsson.
GALERIE STANGL, Munich, February 2-March 20, 1965.
GALERIE CHALETTE, New York, November-December, 1966. Text by I. Myerson and Michel Ragon.

## Selected group exhibitions

MUSEUM OF ART, CARNEGIE INSTITUTE, Pittsburgh, December 5, 1958-February 8, 1959, *The Pittsburgh International Exhibition of Contemporary Painting and Sculpture*.
DOCUMENTA II, Kassel, Germany, July 11-October 11, 1959, *Kunst Nach 1945*.
MUSEUM OF ART, CARNEGIE INSTITUTE, Pittsburgh, October 27, 1961-January 7, 1962, *The Pittsburgh International Exhibition of Contemporary Painting and Sculpture*.
THE SOLOMON R. GUGGENHEIM MUSEUM, New York October 3, 1962-January 6, 1963, *Modern Sculpture from the Joseph H. Hirshhorn Collection*.
SEATTLE WORLD'S FAIR, Seattle, April 21-October 21, 1962, *Art Since 1950*.
XXXII BIENNALE INTERNAZIONALE D'ARTE VENEZIA, Venice, June 20-October 18, 1964.
XXXIII BIENNALE INTERNAZIONALE D'ARTE VENEZIA, Venice, June 18-October 16, 1966. Text on Robert Jacobsen by Ejner Johansson.
EXPO 67, Montreal, Canada, April-October, 1967, *International Exhibition of Contemporary Sculpture*.

## Bibliography

GUÉGUEN, P. "Jacobsen ou l'âge du fer géometrique", *Aujourd'hui*, Boulogne-sur-Siene, vol. 5, no. 26, April, 1960, pp. 28-29.
IONESCO, EUGENE. "Les Poupées de Jacobsen", *XXe Siècle*, Paris, vol. XXII, no. 15, December, 1960, pp. 111-115.
SEUPHOR, M. "Reliefs Construits", *XXe Siècle*, Paris, vol. XXIII, no. 16, May, 1961, p. 29.
MENTZE, E. *Robert Jacobsen*, Copenhagen, Berlingske Forlag, 1961.
JOLY, PIERRE. "Jacobsen, aujourd'hui", *Art International*, Lugano, vol. VIII, no. 3, March 25, 1963, pp. 36-39.
VOLBOUDT, P. "Jacobsen ou le nouvel âge du fer", *XXe Siècle*, Paris, vol. XXV, no. 21, May, 1963, pp. 62-66.
CHEVALIER, D. "Robert Jacobsen", *Aujourd'hui*, Boulogne-sur-Seine, vol. 8, no. 45, April, 1964, p. 28.

# JERZY JARNUSZKIEWICZ

## One-man exhibition.

GALERIA SZTUKI ZPAP, Warsaw, 1966.

## Selected group exhibitions

SYMPOSIUM FORMA VIVA, Ravne, Yugoslavia, 1964.
I BIENNIAL FORM PRZESTRZENNYCH, (I Biennial of Spatial Forms), Elblag, Poland, July 22-August 11, 1965.
MUSÉE RODIN, Paris, June-September, 1966, *3ème Exposition Internationale de Sculpture Contemporaine*.
KUNSTHISTORISCHE MUSEA OPENLUCHT MUSEUM VOOR BEELDHOUWKUNST, Middelheim, Belgium, 1967.
IX BIENAL DE SÃO PAULO, São Paulo, Brazil, 1967.

## Bibliography

BOROWSKI, WEISLAW. "Jerzy Jarnuszkiewicz", *Projekt 3,* Warsaw, no. 53, 1966, pp. 32-37.
OSEKIA, ANDERZEJ. "Sculpture's Source of Unrest", *Poland,* Warsaw, no. 138, February, 1966, pp. 38-39.

## DONALD JUDD

For bibliography and exhibition list see:
LOS ANGELES COUNTY MUSEUM OF ART, Los Angeles, 1967.

### Selected group exhibitions

VIII BIENAL SAO PAULO, São Paulo, Brazil, September-November, 1965.
THE JEWISH MUSEUM, New York, April 27-June 12, 1966, *Primary Structures.*
THE WASHINGTON GALLERY OF MODERN ART, Washington, D.C., May 6-June 25, 1967, *A New Aesthetic.* Text by Barbara Rose.

### Bibliography

JUDD, DONALD. "Sensibility of the Sixties", *Art in America,* New York, vol. 55, no. 1, January, 1967, p. 49.
PEDERSEN, JANE. "Den N. Y. Abstraktion: Don Judd", *Billedkunst,* Hvidovre, Denmark, vol. 2, no. 1, March, 1967, p. 33.

## ELLSWORTH KELLY

For bibliography and exhibition list see:
LOS ANGELES COUNTY MUSEUM OF ART, Los Angeles, 1967.

### One-man exhibitions

GALERIE ARNAUD, Paris, 1951.
GALERIE MAEGHT, Paris, opened November 20, 1964, *Oeuvres récentes de Ellsworth Kelly.*
FERUS GALLERY, Los Angeles, opened March 15, 1966.

### Selected group exhibitions

VI BIENAL DE SÃO PAULO, São Paulo, Brazil, September-December, 1961.
MUSEUM OF ART, CARNEGIE INSTITUTE, Pittsburgh, October 27, 1961-January 7, 1962, *The 1961 Pittsburgh International Exhibition of Contemporary Painting and Sculpture.*
DOCUMENTA III, Kassel, Germany, June 27-October 5, 1964, *Malerei und skulptur.*
MUSEUM OF ART, CARNEGIE INSTITUTE, Pittsburgh, October 30, 1964-January 10, 1965, *The 1964 International Exhibition of Contemporary Painting and Sculpture.*
THE JEWISH MUSEUM, New York, April 27-June 12, 1966, *Primary Structures.*
XXXIII BIENNALE INTERNAZIONALE D'ARTE VENEZIA, Venice, June 18-October 16, 1966.

### Bibliography

ROSE, BARBABA. "The Sculpture of Ellsworth Kelly," *Artforum,* New York, vol. 5, no. 10, Summer 1967, pp. 51-55.

## ZOLTAN KEMENY

For bibliography and exhibition list see:
MUSÉE NATIONAL D'ART MODERNE, Paris, October 22-December 25, 1966, *Zoltan Kemeny.* Text by Bernard Dorival. Circulated to PALAIS DES BEAUX-ARTS, Brussels, January 5-29, 1967. Modified version, TATE GALLERY, London, March 3-April 9, 1967, and WALLRAF-RICHARTZ MUSEUM, Cologne, April 29-June 11, 1967. Text by Alan Bowness.

### Selected group exhibitions

EXPO 67, Montreal, Canada, April-October, 1967, *International Exhibition of Contemporary Sculpture.*

### Bibliography

ROTZLER, W. "Zu den Metallbildern von Zoltan Kemeny," *Werk,* Winterthur, vol. 50, no. 9, September, 1963, pp. 365-370.
CHEVALIER, D. "La sculpture à la Biennale de Venise", *Aujourd 'hui,* Boulogne-sur-Seine, vol. 8, no. 47, October, 1964, pp. 34-39.

## FREDERICK KIESLER

For bibliography and exhibition list see:
THE SOLOMON R. GUGGENHEIM MUSEUM, New York, May-June, 1964, *Frederick Kiesler: Environmental Sculpture.* Texts by Thomas M. Messer and Kiesler.
LOS ANGELES COUNTY MUSEUM OF ART, Los Angeles, 1967.

### One-man exhibitions

RICHARD FEIGEN GALLERY, Chicago, 1967.
YALE UNIVERSITY SCHOOL OF ART AND ARCHITECTURE, New Haven, April 13-May 14, 1967.

### Bibliography

LEVIN, KIM. "Kiesler and Mondrian: Art into Life", *Art News,* New York, vol. 63, no. 3, May, 1964, pp. 38-64+.
KIESLER, FREDERICK. "Notes on Architecture as Sculpture", *Art in America,* New York, vol. 54, no. 3, May, 1966.
KIESLER, FREDERICK. *Inside the Endless House,* New York, Simon and Schuster, 1966.

## PHILLIP KING

For bibliography and exhibition list see:
STEDELIJK MUSEUM, Amsterdam, November 20, 1966-January 15, 1967, *Vormen van de Kleur.* Text by E. de Wilde and W.A.L. Beeren.

### One-man exhibitions

RICHARD FEIGEN GALLERY, New York, April 6-30, 1966.
RICHARD FEIGEN GALLERY, Chicago, September 20-October 15, 1966.
ISAAC DELGADO MUSEUM OF ART, New Orleans, November, 1966.
ROWAN GALLERY, London, 1967.

### Selected group exhibitions

DOCUMENTA III, Kassel, Germany, June 27-October 5, 1964, *Malerei und Skulptur.*

### Bibliography

RUSSELL, JOHN. "Double Portrait: Phillip King and Bridget Riley", *Art in America,* New York, vol. 55, no. 3, May-June, 1967, pp. 98-107.

## STANISLAV KOLÍBAL

For exhibition list see:
NOVÁ SIŇ, Prague, May 18-June 18, 1967, *Stanislav Kolíbal.*

### Selected group exhibitions

OBLASTNÍ GALERIE V OLOMOUCI, Olomouc, Czechoslovakia, August-September, 1965, *Sochařská Bilance 1955-1965.*

## PIOTR KOWALSKI

For Bibliography see:
KUNSTHALLE, Bern, May 4-June 3, 1963, *Piotr Kowalski.*

### Bibliography

*Babel 65,* Paris, no. 1, 1965. Statement by Kowalski.
SYDHOFF, BEATE. "Experiment med Formens Mojlicheter", *Konstrevy,* Stockholm, vol. XLI, no. 1, 1965, pp. 12-15.
SPRING, B. P. "Explosive forms of Piotr Kowalski" *Architectural Forum,* New York, vol. 123, no. 5, December, 1965, pp. 30-35.

## EDWARD KRASINSKI

### One man-exhibition

KRZYSZTOFORY GALLERY, Krakow, Poland, 1965.
Wroclaw, Poland, 1967.

### Selected group exhibitions

MODERN ART GALLERY, Warsaw, 1964, *Konfrontations 64.*
GALLERY EL, Elblag, Poland, 1965, *Konfrontations 65.*
BIENNALE FORM PRZESTRZENNYCH, (I Biennial of Spatial Forms). Elblag, Poland, July 22-August 11, 1965.
GALERIE FOKSAL, Warsaw, 1966.

## KASPAR-THOMAS LENK

For bibliography and exhibition list see:
STEDELIJK MUSEUM, Amsterdam, November 11, 1966-January 15, 1967, *Vormen van de Kleur*. Text by E. de Wilde and W.A.L. Beeren.

### One man-exhibitions

GALERIE RICKE, Kassel, Germany, September, 1966.
FISCHBACH GALLERY, New York, February 18-March 11, 1967.
ROWAN GALLERY, London, April 14-May 4, 1967.
NAVIGLIO 2, GALLERIA D'ARTE, Milan, May 6-16, 1967, *Lenk e Pfahler*. Text by Umbro Apollonio.

### Bibliography

SOMMER, ED. "Letter from Germany", *Art International*, Lugano, vol. X, no. 10, December 20, 1966, p. 37.

## JACQUES LIPCHITZ

For bibliography and exhibition list see:
HAMMACHER, A. M. *Jacques Lipchitz: His Sculpture*, New York, Harry N. Abrams, 1960.

### One-man exhibitions

TATE GALLERY, London, November, 1959. Retrospective.
THE CORCORAN GALLERY OF ART, Washington, D.C., March 12-April 10, 1960, *Jacques Lipchitz: A Retrospective Exhibition of Sculpture and Drawings*. Texts by Adelyn D. Breeskin, Harmann W. Williams, Jr. and Lipchitz. Circulated to THE BALTIMORE MUSEUM OF ART, April 26-May 29, 1960.
OTTO GERSON GALLERY, New York, November 7-December 9, 1961, *Fifty Years: Lipchitz Sculpture*. Circulated to THE ANDREW DICKSON WHITE MUSEUM OF ART, CORNELL UNIVERSITY, Ithaca, January 9-February 11, 1962.
OTTO GERSON GALLERY, New York, March 15-April 16, 1963.
UNIVERSITY OF CALIFORNIA ART GALLERIES, Los Angeles, March 4-April 14, 1963, *Jacques Lipchitz: Fifty Years of Sculpture*. Circulated 1963-1964 to: DENVER ART MUSEUM; FORT WORTH ART CENTER; ALBRIGHT KNOX ART GALLERY, Buffalo; WALKER ART CENTER, Minneapolis; DES MOINES ART CENTER; PHILADELPHIA MUSEUM OF ART; JOSLYN ART MUSEUM, Nebraska.
THE MUSEUM OF MODERN ART, New York, 1963-1964, *Jacques Lipchitz: Bronze Sketches*, circulated to: OTTO GERSON GALLERY, New York; THE CURRIER GALLERY OF ART, Manchester, New Hampshire; ALBRIGHT KNOX ART GALLERY, Buffalo; THE ARTS CLUB OF CHICAGO; THE DETROIT INSTITUTE OF ARTS.
THE J. L. HUDSON GALLERY, Detroit, October 21-November 28, 1964.
NEWARK MUSEUM, Newark, New Jersey, 1965.
BOSTON UNIVERSITY SCHOOL OF FINE AND APPLIED ARTS, March 15-April 16, 1965.
MAKLER GALLERY, Philadelphia, February 1-26, 1966, *Drawings and Bronzes*.
MARLBOROUGH-GERSON GALLERY, New York, April-May, 1966. Texts by Edward F. Fry and Lipchitz. Circulated to DINKELMAN GALLERY, Toronto, April-May, 1967.

### Selected group exhibitions

DOCUMENTA II, Kassel, Germany, July 11-October 11, 1959, *Kunst Nach 1945*.
DOCUMENTA III, Kassel, Germany, June 27-October 5, 1964, *Malerei und Skulptur*.
EXPO 67, Montreal, Canada, April-October, 1967, *International Exhibition of Contemporary Sculpture*.

### Bibliography

WERNER, ALFRED. "Protean Jacques Lipchitz", *The Painter and Sculptor*, London, vol. 4, no. 2, Winter 1959-1960, pp. 11-15.
KUH, KATHERINE. "Conclusions from an Old Cubist", *Art News*, New York, vol. 60, no. 7, November, 1961, pp. 48-49.
SAWIN, MARTICA. "Gonzalez and Lipchitz", *Arts*, New York, vol. 36, no. 5, February, 1962, pp. 14-19.
NORDLAND, GERALD. "Lipchitz: Lively Legend", *Artforum*, San Francisco, vol. 1, no. 12, June, 1963, pp. 38-40.
BORK, BERT VAN. *Lipchitz, the Artist at Work*, New York, Crown Publishers, Inc., 1966. Foreword by Karl Katz, critical evaluation by Alfred Werner.

## BERNARD LUGINBÜHL

### One-man exhibitions

GALERIE RENÉE ZIEGLER, Zurich, 1961.
BORGENICHT GALLERY, New York, April 16-May 7, 1963.
GALERIE RENÉE ZIEGLER, Zurich, April, 1964.
KORNFELD UND KLIPSTEIN, Bern, October 15-November, 1966.
GALERIE RENÉE ZIEGLER, Zurich, December, 1966.

### Selected group exhibitions

XXVII BIENNALE DI VENEZIA, Venice, 1956.
XXXII BIENNALE INTERNAZIONALE D'ARTE VENEZIA, Venice, June 20-October 18, 1964.
3ème EXPOSITION INTERNATIONAL DE SCULPTURE CONTEMPORAINE, Paris, 1966.

### Bibliography

SCHEIDEGGER, ALFRED. "Der Bildhauer Bernard Luginbühl", *Werk*, vol. 47, no. 2, February, 1960, pp. 65-68.
"Zum Projekt von Bernhard Luginbühl für eine Brunnenplastik im Hof", *Werk*, vol. 49, no. 2, February, 1962, pp. 49-50.

## KAREL MALICH

For exhibition list see:
GALERIE NA KARLOVĚ NÁMĚSTÍ, Prague, 1965, *Karel Malich*. Text by Jiří Padrta.

### Selected group exhibitions

GALERIE BENEDIKTA REJTA V LOUNECH, Prague, Spring-Fall 1966, *Konstruktivní tendence*.
MUSEUM FOLKWANG ESSEN, Essen, Germany, October 16-November 27, 1966, *Tschechoslowakische Plastik von 1900 Bis zur Gegenwart*.

## GIACOMO MANZÙ

For bibliography and exhibition list see:
HÜTTINGER, EDUARD. *Giacomo Manzù*, Bodensee, Verlag Amrisevil, 1956.
For bibliography see:
TATE GALLERY, London, October 1-November 6, 1960, *Giacomo Manzù: Sculpture and Drawings*. Text by Carlo L. Ragghianti. Organized by the Arts Council of Great Britain.

### One-man exhibitions

HANOVER GALLERY, London, November 7-December 7, 1956.
WORLD HOUSE GALLERIES, New York, April 24-May 18, 1957, *Manzù: A Selection of Bronzes, Bas-Reliefs, Drawings*. Text by John Rewald.
ALLAN FRUMKIN GALLERY, Chicago, 1958, *Giacomo Manzù, Recent Sculpture*. Text by Joshua C. Taylor.
WORLD HOUSE GALLERIES, New York, April 5-May 7, 1960. Text by Mario Miniaci.
GALERIE IM ERCKER, St. Gallen, Switzerland, April 9-May 31, 1960.
ODYSSIA GALLERY, New York, to December 31, 1964.
PAUL ROSENBERG AND CO., New York, December 6, 1965-January 29, 1966, *Exhibition of Bronze Reliefs for the Door of St. Peter's and Sculpture, Paintings, Drawing by Giacomo Manzù*.

### Selected group exhibitions

XXXI BIENNALE INTERNAZIONALE D'ARTE VENEZIA, Venice, June 16-October 7, 1962.
XXXII BIENNALE INTERNAZIONALE D'ARTE VENEZIA, Venice, June 20-October 18, 1964.
MUSEUM OF ART, CARNEGIE INSTITUTE, Pittsburgh, October 30, 1964-January 10, 1965, *The 1964 Pittsburgh International Exhibition of Contemporary Painting and Sculpture*.
EXPO 67, Montreal, Canada, April-October, 1967, *International Exhibition of Contemporary Sculpture*.

### Bibliography

PAGE, A. F. "Manzù's Bronze Doors", *Detroit Institute Bulletin*, no. 1, Autumn 1961, pp. 10-12.
ELIOT, A. "Manzù, Mason and God, Doors for Saint Peter's Rome", *Art in America*, New York, vol. 53, no. 1, February, 1965, pp. 130-135.
HODIN, J. P. "Giacomo Manzù: The Door of Death", *Studio International*, London, vol. 171, no. 873, January, 1966 pp. 16-19.

## MARINO MARINI

For bibliography and exhibition list see:
PALAZZO VENEZIA, Rome, March 10-June 10, 1966, *Mostra di Marino Marini*. Text by Giovanni Carandente.

### One-man exhibitions

CINCINNATI ART MUSEUM, Cincinnati, Ohio, April-May, 1953, *Marino Marini: Sculpture and Drawings*.
HANOVER GALLERY, London, May 3-June 16, 1956.
LA BOÉTIE, New York, April 21-May 15, 1964.

### Bibliography

"Un monumento di Marino Marini all'Aja", *Domus*, Milan, no. 375, February, 1961, pp. 43-46.
HADZI, M. L. "Report from Rome: with Marino Marini", *Art in America*, New York, vol. 49, no. 3, 1961, pp. 108-110.
RUSSOLI, F. "Le Guerrier de Marino Marini", *XXe Siècle*, Paris, vol. XXV, no. 21, May, 1963, pp. 57-61.
HODIN, J. P. "Marino Marini: Man and Horse, Man and Woman", *Studio International*, London, vol. 167, no. 851, March, 1964, pp. 94-99.
M. N. "Marino: ritratto di Arp", *Domus*, Milan, no. 421, December, 1964, pp. 48-49.
PICA, A. "Marino Marini in Palazzo Venezia", *Domus*, Milan, no. 442, September, 1966, pp. 49-54.

## JOHN MCCRACKEN

For bibliography and exhibition list see:
LOS ANGELES COUNTY MUSEUM OF ART, Los Angeles, 1967.

### One-man exhibitions

ROBERT ELKON GALLERY, New York, April 18-May 5, 1967.
NICHOLAS WILDER GALLERY, Los Angeles, June, 1967.

### Selected group exhibitions

THE WASHINGTON GALLERY OF MODERN ART, Washington, D.C., May 6-June 25, 1967, *A New Aesthetic*. Text by Barbara Rose.

## CLEMENT MEADMORE

For bibliography and exhibition list see:
BYRON GALLERY, New York, January 18-February 11, 1967, *Meadmore*.

### Bibliography

"Sculpture", *Art and Australia*, Sydney, vol. 3, no. 3, January, 1966.
"New York Scene I: Sculpture", "New York Scene II: Color as an Idiom", *Art and Australia*, Sydney, vol. 3, no. 4, March, 1966, pp. 288-291.

## AIKO MIYAWAKI

For exhibition list see:
TOKYO GALLERY, Tokyo, Japan, March 23-April 8, 1967, *Aiko Miyawaki Exhibition*. Text by Yusuke Nakahara.

### Bibliography

GASSIOT-TALBOT, GÉRALD. "Miyawaki," *Cimaise*, Paris, vol. 9, no. 62, November-December, 1962, p. 85.
ROBERTS, COLETTE. "Miyawaki", *Aujourd'hui*, Boulogne-sur-Seine, vol. 8, no. 47, October, 1964, p. 51.

## HENRY MOORE

For bibliography and exhibition list see:
BOWNESS, ALAN ed. *Henry Moore, Sculpture and Drawings, Volume 3, Sculpture 1955-64;* New York, George Wittenborn, Inc., 1965.

### One-man exhibitions

LANDAU GALLERY, Los Angeles, April 21-May 10, 1958, *Sculpture by Henry Moore*.
GALERIE GÉRALD CRAMER, Geneva, December 4, 1962-January 25, 1963, *Henry Moore: Sculptures, Dessins, Estampes*.
M. KNOEDLER AND CO., INC., New York, Summer 1964, *Henry Moore: Early and Recent Sculpture*.
MUSEU DE ARTE MODERNA, Rio de Janeiro, January 21-February 21, 1965. Text by Herbert Read.

ORLEANS GALLERY, New Orleans, July 10-August 1, 1965. Text by Alfred K. Moir.
PHILADELPHIA COLLEGE OF ART, Philadelphia, March 12-April 19, 1966, *Art and Idea: Henry Moore*. Text by Herbert Read.
MARLBOROUGH FINE ART LTD., London, July-August, 1966.
THE ISRAEL MUSEUM, Jerusalem, September-October, 1966, *Henry Moore: Sculptures and Drawings*.
GALLERY MOOS LTD., Toronto, October 29-November 16, 1966.
DE CORDOVA MUSEUM, Lincoln, Massachusetts, January 22-February 19, 1967, *Sculpture and Graphics by Henry Moore*. Exhibition circulated by the Smithsonian Institution.

### Selected group exhibitions

EXPO 67, Montreal, Canada, April-October, 1967, *International Exhibition of Contemporary Sculpture*.

### Bibliography

SELDIS, H. J. "Henry Moore", *Art in America*, New York, vol. 51, no. 5, October, 1963, pp. 56-59.
HALL, DONALD. *Henry Moore: The Life and Work of a Great Sculptor*, New York, Harper & Row, 1966. First published in *The New Yorker*, New York, December 11 and 18, 1965.

## ROBERT MORRIS

For bibliography and exhibition list see:
LOS ANGELES COUNTY MUSEUM OF ART, Los Angeles, 1967.

### One-man exhibition

LEO CASTELLI GALLERY, New York, March 4-28, 1967.

### Selected group exhibitions

THE JEWISH MUSEUM, New York, April 27-June 12, 1966, *Primary Structures*.

### Bibliography

PEDERSEN, JANE. "Den N. Y. Abstraktion: Robert Morris", *Billedkunst*, Hvidovre, Denmark, vol. 2, no. 1, March, 1967, p. 32.
MORRIS, ROBERT. "Notes on Sculpture, Part 3: Notes and Nonsequiturs", *Artforum*, New York, vol. V, no. 10, Summer 1967, pp. 24-29.

## ROBERT MÜLLER

For bibliography and exhibition list see:
KUNSTVEREIN FÜR DIE RHEINLANDE UND WESTFALEN, Düsseldorf, August 6-October 17, 1965, *Robert Müller*. Texts by Karl-Heinz Hering and H. S. Previously shown at: STEDELIJK MUSEUM, Amsterdam; KUNSTHALLE, Bern; PALAIS DE BEAUX-ARTS, Brussels; MUSEUM DES 20. JAHRHUNDERTS, Vienna.

### One-man exhibition

GALERIE DE FRANCE, Paris, January 13-February, 1967.

## ROBERT MURRAY

For bibliography and exhibition list see:
LOS ANGELES COUNTY MUSEUM OF ART, Los Angeles, 1967.

### One-man exhibition

DAVID MIRVISH GALLERY, Toronto, May 4-28, 1967.

### Bibliography

HOLSTEIN, J. "New York's Vitality Tonic for Canadian Artists", *Canadian Art*, Ottawa, issue no. 93, vol. XXI, no. 5, September, 1964, p. 274.
ROSE, B. "Letter from New York: Murray and the New Sculpture", *Canadian Art*, Ottawa, issue no. 98, vol. XXII, no. 4, September-October, 1965, pp. 53-54.
Statement by the artist. "The Education of Twelve Practicing Artists", *Canadian Art*, Ottawa, issue no. 99, vol. XXII, no. 5, November-December, 1965, p. 29.
Statement by the artist. "Ten Artists in Search of Canadian Art", *Canadian Art*, Ottawa, issue no. 100, vol. XXIII, no. 1, January, 1966. p. 65.
SNYDER. ROBERT. "Robert Murray at Bethlehem Steel", *Canadian Art*, Ottawa, issue, no. 102, vol. XXIII, no. 3, July, 1966, pp. 10-11.
ASHTON, DORE. "The Language of Technics", *Arts*, New York, vol. 41, no. 7, May, 1967, p. 11.

# EDGAR NEGRET

For bibliography and exhibition list see:
BIBLIOTECA LUIS-ANGEL ARANGO DEL BANCO DE LA REPUBLICA, Bogotá, March 5-21, 1962, *Negret—Aparatos Mágicos.*

## One-man exhibitions

GALERIA DEL ARTE EL CALLEJON, Bogotá, 1963.
LIBRERIA CENTRAL, Bogotá, 1963.
GRAHAM GALLERY, New York, February 4-29, 1964, *Ramirez and Negret.*
GRAHAM GALLERY, New York, April 26-May 21, 1966.

## Selected group exhibitions

VIII BIENAL DE SÃO PAULO, São Paulo, Brazil, September-November, 1965. Text to Columbian section by Jorge de Oteiza, pp. 180-185.
RICHARD DE MARCO GALLERY, Edinburgh, February-March, 1967.

# LOUISE NEVELSON

For bibliography and exhibition list see:
WHITNEY MUSEUM OF AMERICAN ART, New York, March 8-April 30, 1967, *Louise Nevelson.* Text by John Gordon. Circulated to ROSE ART MUSEUM, BRANDEIS UNIVERSITY, Waltham, Massachusetts, May 24-July 2, 1967.

## One-man exhibitions

GALERIE JEANNE BUCHER, Paris, 1958.
GALERIE SCHWARZ, Milan, April, 1961.
DANIEL CORDIER AND RODOLPHE STADLER GALLERY, Frankfurt-am-Main, January 18-February 28, 1962.
MARTHA JACKSON GALLERY, New York, January 24-February 17, 1962. *Nevelson: Terra Cottas, 1938-1948.*
GALERIE DANIEL GERVIS, Paris, June 7-July 12, 1967

## Selected group exhibitions

LOS ANGELES COUNTY MUSEUM OF ART, Los Angeles, 1967.

## Bibliography

SECKLER, DOROTHY. "The Artist Speaks: Louise Nevelson", *Art in America*, New York, vol 55, no. 1, January, 1967, pp. 32-43.

# ISAMU NOGUCHI

## One-man exhibitions

EUGENE SCHOEN GALLERY, New York, 1929.
MARIE STERNER GALLERY, New York, February, 1930.
BECKER GALLERY, New York, February, 1932.
REINHARDT GALLERIES, New York, December, 1932.
MARIE HARRIMAN GALLERIES, New York, February, 1935.
EGAN GALLERY, New York, March, 1949.
STABLE GALLERY, New York, November 23, 1954-January 8, 1955, *Noguchi: terracottas.*
ARTS CLUB OF CHICAGO, November 11-December 7, 1955, *Noguchi: Sculpture and Scroll Drawings.*
CORDIER-WARREN GALLERY, New York, May 16-June 17, 1961. *New Sculpture.*
FORT WORTH ART CENTER, Fort Worth, Texas, May-July, 1961. *Noguchi: An exhibition of sculpture.*
CORDIER & EKSTROM, INC., New York, April 2-27, 1963. *Noguchi: new bronzes.*
GALERIE CLAUDE BERNARD, Paris, June, 1964. Text by Annette Michelson.
CORDIER & EKSTROM, INC., New York, March 30-April 24, 1965. *Noguchi: stone sculpture.*
CORDIER & EKSTROM, INC., New York, April 4-29, 1967. *New Sculptures.*

## Selected group exhibitions

MUSEUM OF ART, CARNEGIE INSTITUTE, Pittsburgh, *The Pittsburgh International Exhibition of Contemporary Painting and Sculpture:* 1958, 1962, 1965.
I BIENAL DO MUSEU DE ARTE MODERNA DE SÃO PAULO, São Paulo, Brazil, October-December, 1951.
DOCUMENTA II, Kassel, Germany, July 11-October 11, 1959.
DOCUMENTA III, Kassel, Germany, June 27-October 5, 1964.
EXPO 67, Montreal, Canada, April-October, 1967, *International Exhibition of Contemporary Sculpture.*

## Bibliography

LEVY, J. "Isamu Noguchi," *Creative Art*, New York, vol. XII, no. 1, January, 1933, pp. 29-35.
HESS, THOMAS B. "Noguchi '46," *Art News*, New York, vol. 45, no. 7, September, 1946, pp. 34-38+.
NOGUCHI, ISAMU. "Meanings in Modern Sculpture", *Art News*, New York, vol. 48, no. 1, March, 1949, pp. 12-15, 55-56.
NOGUCHI, I. "Nature and enormous potential importance of sculpture, the art of spaces", *Interiors*, New York, vol. CVIII, no. 8, March, 1949, pp. 118-23.
NOGUCHI, I. "Towards a Reintegration of the Arts," *College Art Journal*, vol. 9, no. 1, Autumn 1949, pp. 59-60.
*Noguchi.* Introduction by Shuzo Takiguchi, Saburo Hasegawa, and Isamu Noguchi, Tokyo, Bijutsu Shuppan-sha, 1953.
NOGUCHI, I. "House by Isamu Noguchi: A Living and Working Environment at the Sea", *Arts and Architecture*, Los Angeles, vol. 72, no. 11, November, 1955, pp. 26-27.
PAGE, ADDISON FRANKLIN. "Isamu Noguchi," *Art in America*, New York, vol. 44, no. 4, Winter 1956-57, pp. 24-26, 64-66.
NOGUCHI, ISAMU. "Recently completed gardens of UNESCO headquarters in Paris," *Arts and Architecture*, Los Angeles, vol. 76, no. 1, January, 1959, pp. 12-13.
ASHTON, DORE. "Isamu Noguchi," *Arts and Architecture*, Los Angeles, vol. 76, no. 8, August, 1959, pp. 14-15.
MATHEY, FRANÇOIS. "Le Jardin de Noguchi (at UNESCO headquarters)," *Quadrum*, Brussels, no. 6, 1959, pp. 36-39.
ASHTON, DORE. "Isamu Noguchi," *Arts and Architecture*, Los Angeles, vol. 80, no. 6, June, 1963, pp. 6-7, 30.
NOGUCHI, I. "New stone gardens," *Art in America*, New York, vol. 52, no. 3, June, 1964, pp. 84-89.
ASHTON, D. "Dallo studio di Isamu Noguchi", *Domus*, Milan, no. 415, June, 1964, pp. 52-55.
SPENCER, CHARLES S. "Martha Graham and Noguchi," *Studio International*, London, vol. 173, no. 889, May, 1967, pp. 250-51.

# CLAES OLDENBURG

For bibliography and exhibition list see:
LOS ANGELES COUNTY MUSEUM OF ART, Los Angeles, 1967.

## One-man exhibition

PACE GALLERY, New York, May 10, 1964.

## Selected group exhibitions

XXXII BIENNALE INTERNAZIONALE D'ARTE VENEZIA, Venice, June 20-October 18, 1964. Text on Oldenburg by Alan Solomon, p. 280.

## Bibliography

ROSE, BARBARA. "Claes Oldenburg's Soft Machines", *Artforum*, New York, vol. V, no. 10, Summer 1967, pp. 30-35.

# EDUARDO PAOLOZZI

For bibliography and exhibition list see:
RIJKSMUSEUM KRÖLLER-MÜLLER, Otterlo, Holland, May 7-July 2, 1967, *Eduardo Paolozzi and Anthony Caro.* Text "Theories Concerning Aesthetic Chance and Neo-Plasticism", by Paolozzi.

## One-man exhibition

HANOVER GALLERY, London, June 14-July 21, 1967.

## Selected group exhibitions

XXX BIENNALE INTERNAZIONALE D'ARTE VENEZIA, Venice, 1960. Text on Paolozzi by Robert Melville.
VII BIENAL DE SÃO PAULO, São Paulo, Brazil, September-December, 1963.
LONDON COUNTY COUNCIL, Battersea Park, London, June-September, 1966, *Sculpture in the Open Air.*

## Bibliography

MELVILLE, ROBERT. "Eduardo Paolozzi", *L'Oeil*, Paris, no. 65, May, 1960, pp. 58-63, 81.
BARO, GENE. "A Look at Reminiscence", *Arts*, New York, vol. 38, no. 2, November, 1963, pp. 44-47.
REICHARDT, JASIA. "Eduardo Paolozzi", *Studio International*, London, vol. 168, no. 858, October, 1964, pp. 152-157.
HAMILTON, RICHARD. "Interview with Eduardo Paolozzi", *Contemporary Sculpture: Arts Yearbook 8*, New York, 1965, pp. 160-163.

## GEORG KARL PFAHLER

For bibliography and exhibition list see:
STEDELIJK MUSEUM, Amsterdam, November 20, 1966-January 15, 1967, *Vormen van de Kleur.* Texts by E. de Wilde and W.A.L. Beeren.

### One-man exhibitions

GALERIE MÜLLER, Stuttgart, December 14, 1965-January 20, 1966, *Georg Karl Pfahler, Neue Bilder und Farbraumobjekte.*
NAVIGLIO 2, GALLERIA D'ARTE, Milan, May 6-16, 1967, *Lenk e Pfahler.* Text by Umbro Apollonio.

### Selected group exhibitions

MUSEUM OF ART, CARNEGIE INSTITUTE, Pittsburgh, Fall 1967, *The 1967 Pittsburgh International Exhibition of Contemporary Painting and Sculpture.*

### Bibliography

DE LA MOTTE, MANFRED. "Pfahler: L'Esprit du Réalité", *Art International*, Lugano, vol. VIII, no. 8, October 20, 1964, pp. 44-46.

## PABLO PICASSO

For bibliography and exhibition list of Picasso's sculpture see:
TATE GALLERY, London, June 9-August 13, 1967, *Picasso: Sculpture, Ceramics, Graphic Work.* Organized by the Arts Council of Great Britain. Text by Roland Penrose. Circulated to THE MUSEUM OF MODERN ART, New York, October 9, 1967-January 7, 1968. A complete bibliography on Picasso's sculpture is in preparation for the catalogue of The Museum of Modern Art exhibition.

## VJENCESLAV RICHTER

### One-man exhibition

MUSEJ ZA UMJETNOST I OBRT, Zagreb, April 8-24, 1964.

### Selected group exhibitions

GALERIJA SUVREMENE UMJETNOSTI, Zagreb, August 1-September 15, 1963, *Nove Tendencije 2.*
GALERIJA SUVREMENE UMJETNOSTI, Zagreb, August 13-September 19, 1965, *Nova Tendencija 3.*
VIII BIENNALE DE SÃO PAULO, São Paulo, Brazil, September-November, 1965.

### Bibliography

RICHTER, V. "Izvjestaj br. 1," *A*, Zagreb, May 2, 1963.
RICHTER, V. "Sistemska Plastika," *A*, Zagreb, March 22, 1964.
RICHTER, V. *Sinturbanizam*, Zagreb, Mladost, 1964.

## GEORGE RICKEY

For bibliography and exhibition list see:
LOS ANGELES COUNTY MUSEUM OF ART, Los Angeles, 1967.

### One-man exhibition

STAEMPFLI GALLERY, New York, May 23-June 17, 1967, *George Rickey, Recent Kinetic Sculpture.* Text by George Staempfli. Circulated to WALKER ART CENTER, Minneapolis, Minnesota, July 23-August 27, 1967.

### Bibliography

RICKEY, GEORGE. "Origins of Kinetic Art", *Studio International*, London, vol. 173, no. 886, February, 1967, pp. 65-72.

## KEN SAKAKI

### One-man exhibitions

GALERIE 16, Kyoto, 1962.
GALERIE 16, Kyoto, 1964.
KINDAI TSUBAKI GALLERY, Tokyo, 1965.

## GEORGE SEGAL

For bibliography and exhibition list see:
LOS ANGELES COUNTY MUSEUM OF ART, Los Angeles, 1967.

### One-man exhibitions

SIDNEY JANIS GALLERY, New York, October 4-30, 1965, *New Sculpture by George Segal.*
SIDNEY JANIS GALLERY, New York, March 29-April 22, 1967.

### Bibliography

PINCUS-WITTEN, ROBERT. "George Segal as Realist", *Artforum*, New York, vol. V, no. 10, Summer 1967, pp. 84-87.

## PABLO SERRANO

For bibliography and exhibition list see:
MORENO GALVAN, JOSÉ MARIA. *Pablo Serrano*, New York, Spanish Pavilion, New York World's Fair, 1964-65.

### One-man exhibition

GALERIA JUANA MORDÓ, Madrid, January 10-31, 1967.

## MORIO SHINODA

For bibliography and exhibition list see:
KIKO GALLERIES, Houston, Texas, March 12-March 31, 1967, *Morio Shinoda.* Text by the artist.

## ANTHONY SMITH

For bibliography and exhibition list see:
LOS ANGELES COUNTY MUSEUM OF ART, Los Angeles, 1967.

### One-man exhibition

BRYANT PARK, New York, January 27-February, 1967.

### Selected group exhibitions

THE JEWISH MUSEUM, New York, April 27-June 12, 1966, *Primary Structures.*
DETROIT INSTITUTE OF ARTS, Detroit, April 11-May 21, 1967, *Form, Color, Image.* Text by Gene Baro.
ART INSTITUTE OF CHICAGO, June 23-August 23, 1967, *Sculpture: A Generation of Innovation.*

### Bibliography

BURTON, SCOTT. "Old master at the new frontier," *Art News*, New York, vol. 65, no. 8, December, 1966, pp. 52-55, 68-70.
BARO, GENE. "Tony Smith, Towards Speculation in Pure Form", *Art International*, Zurich, vol. XI, no. 6, Summer, 1967, pp. 27-30.
LIPPARD, LUCY. "Tony Smith 'The Ireluctable' Modality of the Visible", *Art International*, Zurich, vol. XI, no. 6, Summer, 1967, pp. 24-26.

## DAVID SMITH

For bibliography and exhibition list see:
FOGG ART MUSEUM, Cambridge, Massachusetts, September 28-November 15, 1966, *David Smith.* Text by Jane Harrison Cone. Circulated to WASHINGTON GALLERY OF MODERN ART, Washington, D.C., January 7-February 26, 1967.

### One-man exhibitions

HAYDEN GALLERY, Massachusetts Institute of Technology, Cambridge, Massachusetts, February 9-27, 1962, *David Smith: Sculptures and Reliefs.*
MARLBOROUGH-GERSON GALLERY, New York, April-May 1967, *David Smith: Eight Early Works 1935-38.* Text by Rosalind Krauss.

### Selected group exhibitions

LOS ANGELES COUNTY MUSEM OF ART, Los Angeles, 1967.
EXPO 67, Montreal, Canada, April-October, 1967, *International Exhibition of Contemporary Sculpture.*

## Bibliography

MOTHERWELL, ROBERT. "David Smith: A Major American Sculptor", *Studio International*, London, vol. 172, no. 880, August, 1966, pp. 65-68.

BARO, GENE. "David Smith: The Art of Wholeness", *Studio International*, London, vol. 172, no. 880, August, 1966, pp. 69-75

SCHNEEDE, UWE M. "David Smith anlässlich seiner ersten Retrospektive in Europa" *Kunstwerk*, Baden-Baden, vol. 20, nos. 1-2, October-November, 1966, pp. 21-27.

BAYNES, KEN. "Exhibition at the Tate Gallery", *Architectural Review*, London, vol. 140, no. 837, November, 1966, pp. 357-60.

KOZLOFF, MAX. "David Smith at the Tate", *Artforum*, Los Angeles, vol. V, no. 3, November, 1966, pp. 28-30.

CONE, JANE HARRISON. "David Smith", *Artforum*, New York, vol. V, no. 10, Summer 1967, pp. 72-78.

## RICHARD STANKIEWICZ

For exhibition list see:
BOSTON UNIVERSITY ART GALLERY, Boston, March 30-April 30, 1963, *Six Sculptors*. Text by Sam Hunter.

### One-man exhibitions

HANSA GALLERY, New York, December 20, 1954-January 15, 1955.
HANSA GALLERY, New York, December 10-29, 1956.
HANSA GALLERY, New York, December 16, 1957-January 4, 1958.
STABLE GALLERY, New York, January 5-24, 1959.
STABLE GALLERY, New York, April 5-26, 1960.
GALERIE NEUFVILLE, Paris, October 11-November 12, 1960.
STABLE GALLERY, New York, June 5-30, 1961.
PACE GALLERY, Boston, October 23-November 11, 1961.
STABLE GALLERY, New York, April 17-May 5, 1962.
WALKER ART CENTER, Minneapolis, Minnesota, October 21-November 24, 1963.
STABLE GALLERY, New York, March 24-April 18, 1964.
STABLE GALLERY, New York, March 30-April 17, 1965.

### Selected group exhibitions

LONDON COUNTY COUNCIL, Battersea Park, London, May-September, 1963, *Sculpture in the Open Air*.

### Bibliography

PORTER, FAIRFIELD. "Stankiewicz Makes a Sculpture", *Art News*, New York, vol. 54, no. 5, September, 1955, pp. 36-39+.

PEARLSTEIN, P. "Private myth, a symposium", *Art News*, New York, vol. 60, no. 5, September, 1961, pp. 42-44+.

WRIGHT, C. "Stankiewicz: Junk Poet", *Studio International*, London, vol. 164, July, 1962, pp. 2-5.

## JEAN TINGUELY

For bibliography and exhibition list see:
MUSÉE DES ARTS DECORATIFS, Paris, June-September, 1965, *Trois Sculpteurs: César, Roël d'Haese, Tinguely*. Text by James Johnson Sweeney.
THE JEWISH MUSEUM, New York, November 23, 1965-January 2, 1966, *Two Kinetic Sculptors: Nicolas Schöffer and Jean Tinguely*. Texts by Jean Cassou, K. G. Hulten, Sam Hunter. Circulated to: The WASHINGTON GALLERY OF MODERN ART, January 14-February 20, 1966; THE WALKER ART CENTER, Minneapolis, March 7-April 10, 1966; THE CARNEGIE INSTITUTE, Pittsburgh, April 28-May 29, 1966; THE CONTEMPORARY ART COUNCIL OF THE SEATTLE MUSEUM, June 27-July 31, 1966.

### One-man exhibitions

GIMPEL AND HANOVER GALERIE, Zurich, October 12-November, 1966.
GALERIE ALEXANDRE IOLAS, Paris, June 1967.

### Bibliography

AMMAN, JEAN-CHRISTOPHE. "Jean Tinguely", *Werk*, Winterthur, vol. 53, no. 3, March, 1966, pp. 112-120.

JOUFFROY, ALAIN. "Jean Tinguely", *L'Oeil*, Paris, no. 136, April, 1966, pp. 34-43+.

BILLETER, FRITZ. "Interview mit Jean Tinguely", *Kunstwerk*, Baden-Baden, vol. 20, nos. 9-10, June-July, 1967, pp. 15-23.

## HAROLD TOVISH

For bibliography and exhibition list see:
TERRY DINTENFASS GALLERY, New York, March 2-27, 1965. *Harold Tovish*.

### One-man exhibitions

SWETZOFF GALLERY, Boston, April 12-May 1, 1965.
WATSON GALLERY, Norton, Massachusetts, March 3-April 16, 1967. *Harold Tovish, Twenty Years of Sculpture—1946-1966*. Text by H. Haarvard Arnason.

### Selected group exhibitions

XXVIII BIENNALE DI VENEZIA, Venice, June 16-October 21, 1956.

### Bibliography

TOVISH, HAROLD. "Sculpture: the Sober Art", *The Atlantic Monthly*, Boston, vol. 206, no. 3, September, 1961, pp. 35-39.

## ERNEST TROVA

For bibliography and exhibition list see:
PACE GALLERY, New York, January 14-February 11, 1967, *Recent sculpture by Ernest Trova*. Text by Lawrence Alloway. Also shown at HAYDEN GALLERY, Massachusetts Institute of Technology, Cambridge, Feburary 20-March 19, 1967.

### Selected group exhibitions

LOS ANGELES COUNTY MUSEUM OF ART, Los Angeles, 1967.

## DRAGO TRŠAR

For bibliography and exhibition list see:
KRŽIŠNIK, ZORAN. *Drago Trsar*, Ljubljana Salon, Moderne Galerije, 1962.

### One-man exhibitions

MALA-GALERIJA, Ljubljana, November, 1960.
MALA-GALERIJA, Ljubljana, May, 1964.

### Selected group exhibitions

MUSÉE RODIN, Paris, Summer 1956, *Exposition Internationale de Sculpture Contemporaine*.
KUNSTHISTORISCHE MUSEA OPENLUCHTMUSEUM VOOR BEELDHOUWKUNST, Middelheim, June 20-September 30, 1965, *8 Biennale voor Beeldehouwkunst*.

## WILLIAM TUCKER

For exhibition list see:
THE JEWISH MUSEUM, New York, April 27-June 12, 1966, *Primary Structures*.

### One-man exhibitions

RICHARD FEIGEN GALLERY, New York, November 31-December 30, 1965.
ROWAN GALLERY, London, 1966.
KASMIN GALLERY, London, 1967.

### Selected group exhibitions

LONDON COUNTY COUNCIL, Battersea Park, London, June-September 1966, *Sculpture in the Open Air*.
5e INTERNATIONALE BEELDENTENTOONSTELLING, Sonsbeek, The Netherlands, May 27-September 25, 1966.

### Bibliography

BARO, GENE. "Britain's Young Sculptors", *Arts*, New York, no. 40, no. 2, December, 1955, pp. 14-17.

REICHARDT, JASIA. "Colour in Sculpture", *Quadrum*, Brussels, vol. 18, 1965, pp. 75-77.

DIENST, ROLF-GUNTER. "Drei Aspekte der Neuen Englischen Plastik", *Kunstwerk*, Baden-Baden, vol. 19, no. 9, March, 1966, pp. 11-15.

## WILLIAM TURNBULL

For bibliography and exhibition list see:
NEWPORT HARBOR PAVILION GALLERY, Balboa, California, March 13-April 24, 1966. Text by Jules Langsner.

### One-man exhibition

THE WADDINGTON GALLERIES, London, April 4-29, 1967.

### Selected group exhibitions

STEDELIJK MUSEUM, Amsterdam, November 20, 1966-January 15, 1967, *Vormen van de Kleur*. Texts by E. de Wilde and W. A. L. Beeren.
LONDON COUNTY COUNCIL, Battersea Park, London, June-September 1966, *Scultpure in the Open Air*.

### Bibliography

TURNBULL, WILLIAM. "Images without Temples", *Living Arts I*, London, The Institute of Contemporary Arts, 1963, pp. 14-27.
BARO, GENE. "Changed Englishman, William Turnbull", *Art in America*, New York, vol. 54, no. 2, March, 1966, pp. 102-103.

## FRITZ WOTRUBA

For bibliography and exhibition list see:
*Fritz Wotruba*, Neuchatel, Switzerland, Editions du Griffon, 1961. Introduction by Friedrich Heer. English translation by Peter Foges and Haakon Chevalier.

### One-man exhibitions

GALERIE CHARLES LIENHARD, Zurich, March 19-April, 1963. Text by Rudolf Wach.
MUSEUM DES 20.JAHRHUNDERTS, Vienna, May 17-June 25, 1963.
MARLBOROUGH-GERSON GALLERY, New York, March 9, 1964.

### Selected group exhibitions

THE SOLOMON R. GUGGENHEIM MUSEUM, New York, October 3, 1962-January 6, 1963, *Modern Sculpture from the Joseph H. Hirshhorn Collection*.
DOCUMENTA III, Kassel, Germany, June 27-October 5, 1964, *Malerei und Skulptur*.
EXPO 67, Montreal, Canada, April-October, 1967, *International Exhibition of Contemporary Sculpture*.

### Bibliography

CSOKOR, F. T. "Umsturz im Bühnenbild: Fritz Wotruba und Oskar Kokoschka", *Kunstwerk*, Baden-Baden, vol. 4, no. XIV, October, 1960, pp. 18-37.
KRAMER, H. "Notes on Wotruba and Spaventa", *Arts*, New York, vol 38, no. 7, April, 1964, pp. 16-20.
BREICHA, O. "Fritz Wotrubas Relief in Marburg an der Lahn", *Werk*, Winterthur, vol. 52, no. 5, May, 1965, pp. 188-191.
BREICHA, OTTO. "The New Austrian Sculpture" *Studio International*, London, vol. 170, no. 872, December, 1965, pp. 220-228.

## KATSUHIRO YAMAGUCHI

For exhibition list see:
THE MUSEUM OF MODERN ART, New York, October 17-December 26, 1966. *The New Japanese Painting and Sculpture*. Text by William S. Lieberman.

## KAZUO YUHARA

### Selected group exhibitions

MUSÉE D'ART MODERNE DE LA VILLE DE PARIS, Paris, September 28-November 3, 1965, *IVème Biennale de Paris*.
MUSÉE RODIN, Paris, April 29-May 30, 1965, *XVIIème Salon de la Jeune Sculpture*.
THE TOKYO METROPOLITAN ART GALLERY, Tokyo, May 10-31, 1967, *The IX Tokyo Biennale*.

### Bibliography

YUHARA, KAZUO. "Sculpture and I", *Today's Eyes, The News of the National Modern Art Museum of Tokyo*, Tokyo, no. 102, 1963. (Text in Japanese).
TONO, Y. "Exhibition Color and Space", *Bijitutecho*, no. 276, 1966. (Text in Japanese).
YUHARA, KAZUO. "Review: Exhibition of Two Decades of American Painting", *Bijitutecho*, no. 276, 1966. (Text in Japanese).

# INDEX OF ARTISTS

| | | | |
|---|---|---|---|
| **Australia** | Meadmore | **Spain** | Picasso |
| | | | Serrano |
| **Austria** | Wotruba | | Chillida |
| | Hoflehner | | |
| | | **Switzerland** | Arp |
| **Belgium** | d'Haese | | Giacometti |
| | Bury | | Kemeny |
| | | | Bill |
| **Canada** | Bladen | | Müller |
| | Murray | | Tinguely |
| | | | Luginbühl |
| **Colombia** | Negret | | |
| | | **United Kingdom** | Moore |
| **Czechoslovakia** | Malich | | Hepworth |
| | Kolibal | | Armitage |
| | | | Turnbull |
| **Denmark** | Jacobsen | | Caro |
| | | | Paolozzi |
| **France** | Etienne-Martin | | King |
| | Ipousteguy | | Tucker |
| | César | | |
| | Kowalski | | |
| | | **United States** | Lipchitz |
| **Germany** | Haese | | Kiesler |
| | Pfahler | | Calder |
| | Lenk | | Nevelson |
| | | | Noguchi |
| **Israel** | Ben-Schmuel | | Diller |
| | | | Smith, A. |
| **Italy** | Colla | | Smith, D. |
| | Fontana | | Rickey |
| | Marini | | Agostini |
| | Manzù | | Tovish |
| | Cascella, A. | | Stankiewicz |
| | Consagra | | Kelly |
| | | | Segal |
| **Japan** | Horiuti | | Chamberlain |
| | Yamaguchi | | Trova |
| | Miyawaki | | Judd |
| | Yuhara | | Oldenburg |
| | Shinoda | | Morris |
| | Sakaki | | Di Suvero |
| | Fukushima | | McCracken |
| | | | Bell |
| **Netherlands** | Couzijn | | |
| | | **Yugoslavia** | Richter |
| **Poland** | Jarnuskiewicz | | Tršar |
| | Krasinski | | |

INVENTORY 74

COMPLETED

INVENTORY 1983